The Ritual Year in Ancient Egypt
(Ombos recension)

Lunar & Solar Calendars and Liturgy

by Mogg Morgan

Mandrake

Copyright © Mogg Morgan and Mandrake of Oxford
2011 as *Wheel of the Year in Ancient Egypt*
This impression 2014

All rights reserved. No part of this work may be reproduced or utilized in any form by any means electronic or mechanical, including *xerography, photocopying, microfilm,* and *recording,* or by any information storage system without permission in writing from the author.

Published by
Mandrake of Oxford
PO Box 250
OXFORD
OX1 1AP (UK)
ISBN 978-1-906958-13-8

A Note on Pronunciation

The Egyptian language consistently ignored vowels so by convention and for convenience of pronunciation English vowel 'e' is inserted between each consonant apart from a & A where 'a' is pronounced as in French.

The Egyptian god *Set* is often written in its Hellenised form *Seth* (see *The Bull of Ombos* for discussion). In what follows I have often retained the original Egyptian *Set* for ease of pronunciation, especially in sections destined to be spoken aloud.

Contents

0 Preface - a contemporary round
   of the kemetic ritual year 7

1 The Archaic Lunar Calendar:
   Feasts, liturgy, prayers, hymns and spells 37
   Sutekh 40
   Min 50
   Hathor, Bat, Horus & Seth 57
   Sokar 63
   Neith 67
   Nuit 73
   Wepwawet/Anubis 79
   Renenutet 89
   Khonsu 95
   Khenty-Khet/Horus 100
   Ipet/Hippo Goddess 105
   Ra 110
   Thoth 120

2 The Later Festival Calendar 130
   Basic concepts, weeks, months etc 131
   Month names 133
   Three Seasons 134
   Egyptian Festival Year 135
   Reconstructed Festival Calendar 143
   Epagomenal days 156

3 Lunar-Stellar Calendar of Horus & Seth 163
   The Lunar Calendar 165
   Sirius & the Lunar-Stellar Calendar 168

	How did the Lunar Calendar work?	175
	The Lunar month	176
	The Lunar Year	176
	The Northern Lunar-Solar calendar	180
	Lunar-Stellar or Lunar-Sothic Calendar	185
4	Deities attending the Northern Constellations - the Lunar days	192
	Deities of the waxing or 'Bright' half of the month.	197
	Deities of the waning or 'Dark' half of the month.	204
5	Oracles & Lunar Omina	213
	Appendix: Lunar observations	225
Appendix 1	Lunar diary	239
	Bibliography	242
	Glossary	255
	Index	265

Tables

In Chapter1
Table 1:   Rituals for thirteen Lunar Months 39

In Chapter2
Table 2:   The Ancient Egyptian Civil Year 136
Table 3:   The Festival Year 141

In Chapter 3
Table 4:   Calendar of Medical Papyrus Ebers 171
Table 5:   Papyrus Ebers detail 174
Table 6:   Names of the Lunar Days 178

In Chapter 4
Table 7:   Gods and Festivals of the Lunar Month 199-200
Table 8:   Lunar days from Senmut's tomb 202

Figures

In Chapter 1

Figure 1:	Sutekh of the Hibis Oasis	42
Figure 2:	Min	51
Figure 3:	Hathor, Bat, Horus & Seth	55-6
Figure 4:	Sokar	61-2
Figure 5:	Neith	66
Figure 6:	Nuit	72
Figure 7:	Wepwawet/Anubis	77-8
Figure 8:	Renenutet	88
Figure 9:	Khonsu	94, 98
Figure 10:	Khenty-Khet/Horus	99
Figure 11:	Ipet/Hippo Goddess	104
Figure 12:	Ra	109
Figure 13:	Thoth	121
Figure 14:	Astronomical ceiling from Ramesseum.	127

In Chapter 3

Figure 15:	Ebers calendar	170
Figure 16:	The stars of the Milky Way	183

In Chapter 4

Figure 17:	Astronomical ceiling of Senmut festivals.	196
Figure 18:	Astrological frieze from Edfu	210-12

In Chapter 5

Figure 19:	Oracular Judgement Stele	215
Figure 20:	Dakhleh Stele	217

Acknowledgements

Once again to the staff of the Sackler Library / Griffith Institute, Oxford, that has been my informal 'House of Life' during the writing of this book. To Dr Kurt Locher for supplying copies of his paper "New arguments for the celestial location of the decanal belt and for the origins of the $S3ḥ$ hieroglyph" & "Middle Kingdom Astronomical Coffin Lids" and the idea that one should not be too conservative about the possibility of identifying ancient Egyptian constellations. To Carolyn Graves-Brown of Swansea University for clarification of the idea of the "sun at midnight" in her article on "Flint in the Northern Sky" published in *Egyptian Stories: a tribute to Alan B Lloyd* (2007) edited by T Schneider and Kasia Szpakowska. To Marco Rossani of the Museo delle Antichità Egizie di Torino for help finding the unusual image of Egyptian moon god Khonsu.

To Kym, amanuensis, proof-reader and editor extraordinaire. To the Companions of Set, who have offered useful feedback on many aspects of the work.

Preface

In my previous book *Supernatural Assault in Ancient Egypt* the whole of the second part was dedicated to a reconstructed Egyptian calendar. This material is relevant to the whole of the Egyptian magical religion and thus needed publishing in its own right not merely as an appendix to the Lunar Mysteries of Horus & Set.

The cosmic tides ebb and flow through us every bit as much as they did our Ancient Egyptian ancestors. Over the millennia we have lost contact with them and are alienated from nature. Ironically it was the Egyptians who set this trend in motion when they, in ancient times, reformed the wheel of the year - tearing it from its natural anchors.

Several journals asked me to prepare monthly summaries and these I reprint here as a *taster* to the more in depth material. Some of the calculations of gods' birthdays, horoscopes, etc., need to be redone for each year. This data will be updated on website www.ombos.co.uk and www.scribd.com/ombos

January . . . unsettled by rampant Hippos
Let's face it, after all the excitement of Yule and the secular new year, January in the northern hemisphere is a bit of a downer. But on the basis of forewarned is forearmed. . . knowing this as a time when the cosmic tides are in a difficult point of transition, won't make the winter blues go away but it may help to know the situation is not permanent. These days I find myself teaching in various milieux: as an outreach tutor trying to tempt people back

into education; or ad hoc for an American college in Oxford where I've just completed a course on Hermeticism. It's one of the first things I learnt as a trainee teacher – prepare the student for the downs as well as ups of their journey.

Which brings me then to a quick look at the ancient Egyptian calendar, where our January roughly corresponds with the third month of their winter or "Peret". Traditionally this month was called in Greek "Pharmenoth" - or its older name "Rekh-Nedjes", from when Egypt followed a strictly lunar year. "Rekh-Nedjes" was a reprise of the previous month's fire festivals although on a smaller scale; so you still get the distinct impression of treading on water.

"Pharmenoth" is undoubtedly a Greek rendering of ancient Egyptian "p n jemen hetep" meaning "The One of Amenhotep". Amenhotep is NOT one of Egypt's venerable old gods but a real flesh and blood king, who was so popular than he was eventually immortalized, his name becoming synonymous with the whole month. Which provides a clear example of what scholars call euphemerism – i.e. that some gods are really deified humans. Euphemius was a Greek mythographer whose ideas resonate with those of Hermeticism, summarized as "Blessed are the pure in heart for they shall BE god!"

So what did King Amenhotep do to earn himself the rare honour of reification in the Ancient Egyptian calendar? For that one must look to Egypt's "Second Intermediate period" (c1630-1520BCE), when the "Black Land" was invaded and conquered by an Iron

Age culture called the Hyksos or Shepherd Kings. You can read a lively account of this in Wilbur Smith's novel "River God". The Hyksos prevailed because of their use of iron weapons and wheeled horse drawn chariots all of which they introduced to Bronze Age Egypt. Egypt repaid the gift, perfecting the technology and turning it on their conquerors, eventually driving them from its land and indeed history.

All this is, by the way, hundred of years before Egypt's most famous king Rameses II. Rameses is often mistaken for the supposed hardhearted Pharaoh of the Bible. But from the point of view of the Hysos, Amenhotep would fit that role better than Rameses. Amenhotep I (1545-1525BCE) was the second king of the 18th Dynasty. He consolidated and strengthened his father Ahmose's achievements, driving the Hyksos from Northern Egypt. Amenhotep reigned over a golden age of arts and culture and was venerated as a local god at the craftsmen's colony at Deir el Medina. By the 20th Dynasty his cult had become so popular it gave its name to the entire month.

The Hyksos legacy perhaps survives in ancient Palestine, into whose primitive melting pot they eventually dissolved. In Palestine they contributed some Egyptian elements to the iconography of Hebrew religion. The Hyksos were famous for their adherence to the very ancient Egypt god of intoxication – Set – and there are some correspondences between the Red God and the later cult of Baal and indeed Jahweh. So perhaps all those confused memories in the Bible about a people leaving Egypt owe something to the expulsion of the "Hyksos" or Shepherd Kings from Egypt?

So if you find yourself feeling blue, think about those Ancient Egyptians, who on the threshold of a big change, were still getting angry complaints from their "Hyksos" overlords, who were unable to sleep because of the wailing of the rampant hippos of the Nile.

February . . . Cool for Cats

It's the final of months of winter – hurrah! In Ancient Egypt this was called "Pharmuthi, - the one of Renenutet". Renenutet (Greek Thermouthis) was a harvest goddess, usually depicted as a woman wearing the serpentine uraeus headdress, or as a large snake wearing the solar disk and cow's horns. No doubt Renenutet got her snakey form because of some pragmatic connection with harvested fields – a natural hazard that requires some form of propitiation? But it's remarkable how commonly these dangerous reptiles crop up in Egyptian iconography. Makes you wonder whether there wasn't some form of ancient snake cult behind the scenes somewhere. Sometimes they are colossal, and barely tamed versions of formerly "demonic" avatars.

However, rather strangely, we have to wait to the first day of next month for any special celebrations of Renenutet. I say strange because one kind of expects a deity's festival would be celebrated in the month to which it gives the name. This anachronism is part of the evidence that the Egypt's ritual year was once wholly lunar in character – but more of this later in the book.

Instead, it's a time to feast the Theban cat-goddess *Bastet who was feted* during this month. Snakes and Cats can after all have a dialectical relationship. It's said that in some climes, you choose whether to live with one or the other - cats control the rodents, which would otherwise attract the snakes.

Here are some little snippets from Robert Westall's *Cat's Whispers and Tales*:

> *Best Mouser*: Tortoiseshell called Towser, Glenturret Distillery, Crieff, Tayside. Three mice a day. By the time she was 21 in 1984, 23,000 mice.
> *Best Ratter*: Female tabby called Minnie. White City Stadium, London, 12,480 rats between 1927 and 1932. (Methinks ratters have a shorter lifespan)
> In the *Laws of Hywell Dda*, King of South Wales 936CE one reads:
> "The worth of a cat is this – the worth of a kitten from the night it is kittened until it shall open its eyes is one legal penny. And from that time till it shall kill mice, two legal pence. And after it shall kill mice, four legal pence, and so shall it always remain."
> "The value of a cat which guards a king's barn, if it is killed or stolen (equals) a sheep with her lamb and wool"

So look after our furry friends – and give them an extra treat for the time of year. Ancient Egypt has many myths and stories connected with the cat and her divine personification. The Greek historian Herodotus (Book II. 60-61) gives one of the liveliest accounts of the celebrations at Bubastis (just north of Cairo), in Lower Egypt:

When the people are on their way to Bubastis they go by river, men and women together, a great number of each in every boat. Some of the women make a noise with rattles, others play flutes all the way, while the rest of the women, and the men, sing and clap their hands. As they journey by river to Bubastis, whenever they come near any other town they bring their boat near the bank; then some of the women do as I have said, while some shout mockery of the women of the town; others dance, and others stand up and expose themselves. This they do whenever they come beside any riverside town. But when they have reached Bubastis, they make a festival with great sacrifices, and more wine is drunk at this feast than in the whole year beside. Men and women (but not children) are wont to assemble there to the number of seven hundred thousand, as the people of the place say.

Quite a party – and maybe not what you'd expect of the ritual doings of those stately Egyptians. But there again, much of what you read about Egypt ain't necessarily so.

March ...The first Spring of Summer

For the Ancient Egyptians this would indeed be the first month of the summer (Shemu) season, and was known as "Pachons" – from p-n-khonsu – "the one of Khonsu". Khonsu is the moon god – his name means the Wanderer – an obvious reference to the moon's fast moving and irregular course. Egyptian lunar deities are invariably male – e.g. Thoth, Horus & Seth, and Yael. Which shows there is no simple equation of males being solar, females lunar, of a kind sometimes encountered in Neo-Pagan theology.

The strange thing is, that despite the fact that from time immemorial, this month has been dedicated to the moon god Khonsu, there is no actual record from any period of seasonal rites dedicated to his cult. I suppose we have to assume that they were there but no records have survived, in part because the Egyptians downgraded or abandoned their ancient lunar calendar such a long time ago.

Khonsu, portrayed as a hawk-headed human mummy, holds the scepter and flail, and sports the lopsided hairdo symbolic of youth. His headdress shows the full and crescent moon. The Egyptians often represented their gods as triads – mother, father and offspring. For some he was a cosmological god in his own right - at Kom Ombo the child of crocodile god Sobek and Hathor. But he is more famously part of the so-called Theban triad, the son of Amun the mysterious, "all father"; his mother the archetypal mother "Mut", vulture goddess (not to be confused with Maat, whose emblem is the ostrich feather). I suspect this latter case of mistaken identity stems from an over reliance on the very antiquated works on comparative religion written by Gerald Massey (1828-1907). For example the interesting, if flawed, film "Zeitgeist: The Movie", cites Gerald Massey as pretty much its only authority on ancient religion!

Like many of the famous gods and goddesses of Egypt, Khonsu has a dark side. He can be violent, appearing in the Pyramid Text's enigmatic *Cannibal Hymn*:

> "Indeed, Khonsu (the moon), who slaughters the lords,
> cuts their throats for the King
> and takes out for him what is in their bellies,
> Khonsu is the messenger whom he sends out to chastise."

Which is maybe a reminder that the Moon can be a malign or

sinister force. In classical Paganism, "white" or dayside magick would best be done on the new or dark moon. That's to say done in the absence or "seizure of the moon". That might be the opposite of what you'd expect. But there again in modern witchcraft the new moon is a time to plant a seed, the beginning of the "bright fortnight". The full moon marks the point where things can begin to shrink away, the beginning of the dark. In my book *Supernatural Assault in Ancient Egypt* I discuss the gods Horus and Set, who once personified the important duality of waxing and waning moon. I show that in any month, Set's special days will be on, or around the full moon, white nights and sixteenth day. Whereas Horus, often viewed as the good guy, lurks with his father Osiris around the new moon.

Not surprisingly then Khonsu, is often used in curses, either to send or fend them off. Every Ancient Egyptian child was equipped in their crib with a special decree from the gods. This serves both as natal horoscope and amulet and was worn during the crucial early years as a necklace. It guaranteed the infant's safety from a whole list of malign influences. Khonsu is the key player, both as agent and culprit in the contract (quoted here from my above-mentioned book:)

> "We, Khonsu-who-was-a-Child and Khonsu-the-contriver,
> Those two great living Baboons who rest on the right and Left of Khonsu in Thebes and who are those who issue a book of death and life.
> We shall keep her safe from Sekhmet and her son.
> We shall keep her safe from the collapse of a wall and from the fall of a thunderbolt.
> We shall keep her safe from leprosy, from blindness, and

from the eyes of the undead.
We shall keep her safe from the seven stars of the Great Bear and we shall keep her safe from the star which falls from the sky and strikes one down.
We shall keep her safe from the Company of Heaven; and their abominations;
. . .
We shall keep her safe from the *Books of the beginning of the year*
and from the *Books of the end of the year.*
. . .
We shall keep her safe from the manifestations of Amun, Mut, Montu and Maat and Khonsu"

April . . . Jacob's Ladder

This month of April (II Shemu/Payni) was especially sacred to the Ancient Egyptian god Horus. The falcon god has a confusing variety of forms, but one that is particularly associated with this month is a blind form of Horus - Khenty Irty - also known as Khenty-Khem – 'Foremost of Khem'. His city was known by the Greeks as Letopolis, the 'City of Leto' which is possibly related to "lethe" (oblivion) or lotus, the fruit that brings oblivion to those who eat it. It is a place that has strong associations with ancient stellar magick.

If you have trouble with demons then Letopolis was the place to send them. So in one spell it says 'Your heart is destined for the sacrificial meal of the cobra goddess.' Letopolis is a place to be called to mind whenever one has Typhonian demons that need to be cooked and eaten!

Very little remains of Letopolis, but it is obviously one of those places that in *very* early times was as much a stronghold of Set as it was Horus. The nome standard or 'Totem' of Khem is the Khapesh or Bull's Leg or in later times the constellation of the Great Bear. This constellation is a symbolic representation of Seth. The four stars that form the 'enclosure' of the constellation the Great Bear, are also called the Four Sons of Horus.

Letopolis owes its existence to a special natural phenomenon - connected with meteorites. Letopolis is one of several such 'thunderbolt cities'. There is also a strong association between meteorites and oracular dreams. Thunderbolts, meteorites and arrows from heaven should all remind us of Set, who is sometimes shown with an arrowlike tail.

During the time of the Ramessides (c 1300BCE), the consultation of oracles became very popular. The gods were said to express their will directly to the plaintiff via oracles. Some people speculate that there was a time in the second millenia BCE, when the number of meteorites hitting the Earth was much higher than it is today. Could this be an explanation for the preponderance of thunderbolt mythology all over this region? When scholars looked at the local geology of Letopolis, especially the incidence of fossils, they found another possible explanation for the thunderbolt imagery. In the ancient world, fossils were often connected with thunderbolts and meteorites. And indeed there is a large 'thunderbolt' fossil (*Nerinea Requieniana*) very common in the area and unknown elsewhere.

In the Old Testament's account of 'Jacob's ladder' - we read that Jacob slept with a meteorite for a pillow and as a consequence, enjoyed a visionary dream of angels ascending and descending a heavenly ladder:

> 'Taking one of the stones of the place, he put it under his head and lay down to sleep. And he dreamed that there was a ladder set up on the Earth, and the top of it reached to heaven; and behold, the angels of God were ascending and descending on it!. . . So Jacob rose early in the morning, and he took the stone which he had put under his head and set it up for a pillar and poured oil on top of it. He called the name of that place Bethel.'

Such a dream might also be had in Letopolis. It was a place of ascent with its own ladder, or 'stairway to heaven', constructed from or held up by Set or sometimes Horus and Set. Here it was thought especially likely that the justified could ascend to the imperishable stars. It was also a place where one's inner motives were tested to destruction.

So what happened at the Festival of Letopolis? The celebrated Egyptologist and folklorist Gerald Averay Wainwright speculated that the rites involved some form of fire walking, whereby one was literally tested in the flames just as happened to Shadrach, Meshach and Abednego in the Old Testament *Book of Daniel*.

The future is bleak for those that fail the test - cooked and offered up as food to the city's cannibalistic inhabitants especially Horus the Elder, a cannibal especially fond of blood. It also shows that Seth, who is usually seen as the one who controls and sends the demons and vampires to do his bidding, is also involved in the process of their disposal! Thus in Egyptian religion, no evil is ever absolute.

May . . . Hippo Goddess

Our journey through the reconstructed Egyptian calendar brings us now to the third month of the year known as Epiphi in Greek – Ipet in Egyptian and therefore named after the ancient hippopotamus goddess. She has in fact several names or epithets - Tawaret, which means "great goddess", Ipet which means "harem" or Reret Weret which means "Great Sow". It's as well to bear in mind that hippos are fearsome beasts. Check out the natural history of animal gods, it can often be revealing. It tells us the origin of term "sweating blood' from the blood red secretion that forms part of the hippo's natural protection against the sun. "Hippos are among the most irascible creatures on the continent. While they are typically content to sleep away the day on the shore of a river or in the shallows, when alarmed they are quick to show their hostile side. Hippos are reputed to *cause more human deaths than any other large animal in Africa* (Matrix.com). It all speaks volumes about the way our ancestors related to the dangers of the natural world. Hippos may be pink but they definitely aren't cuddly!

The Egyptians regarded the female hippo as the more benign half of the species with strong maternal instincts; hence her role as protectress of childbirth. The Hippopotamus was also the totemic animal of Seth and Tawaret his "concubine", perhaps because of her abilities to rein in his violent, chaotic nature. The "Book of Day and Night" (from the time of Rameses VI) tells us: "as to this Foreleg of Set, it is in the northern sky, tied to two mooring posts of flint by a chain of gold. Isis, in her hippopotamus form (reret) is tasked with guarding it."

The more aggressive males were the hunter's prey, the ultimate test of male machismo. There are very many inscriptions and texts, which show that the hippopotamus is the most common form adopted by Set when fighting Horus. Perhaps one of the most famous images comes from Edfu, where Horus is the formidable guardian at the gate of the sanctuary, with the testicles of Set in his hand, a victorious god inspiring the demons with terror. Finally, in the Horus myth of Edfu we find the story of the actual fight and the castration of Seth as a hippopotamus:

> "The seventh harpoon is struck fast in his body and hath spiked his testicles." The relief illustrating this text shows Horus thrusting a seventh harpoon into the testicles of the hippopotamus that represents Set. "And after he had cut out his fore-leg *he* threw it into the sky. Spirits guard it there: The Great Bear of the northern sky. The great hippopotamus goddess keeps hold of it, so that it can no longer sail in the midst of the gods." *Pap. Jumilhac* XVII, 11-12)

The Edfu myth represents a *sectarian* version of events and there undoubtedly was an original, more erotic, what we would call *tantrik*, version of the same incident. In my book *Tankhem*, I describe some ancient rites with strong Sethian associations. So for example the gestures of the Heptagram rite may well be an enactment of the above scene from Edfu - Horus leveling his harpoon at Set - Set rising up to the stars.

The pre-dynastic graves of Nagada, excavated by Flinders Petrie and his colleagues tell a slightly different story. Amongst the many thousands of small grave goods, images of the aquatic, 'baying' hippopotamus was one of the most popular. Also common were special flint knives that may have been used to cut the newborn infant's umbilical cord and clear the way for new life to begin. In an odd piece of word play, the name given to the umbilical cord is the same as for the demon of non-being "Apophis". In another myth Apophis is a colossal serpent that threaten the rebirth of the sun god Ra. Set is the ferocious power of Ra, sent to defeat this threat to creation. We can surmise that in the original story, both male and female hippo, though capable of violence, could be helpful in times of crisis.

June . . . Birth of the Sun

This month corresponds with Ancient Egyptian Meso-re – meaning "Birth of Ra" the sun god and this seems appropriate enough for the month of the solstice, although there are other traditions in Egypt that place this in the winter rather than the summer. It's a very pivotal month in more ways than one, it coincides with the heliacal rising of the dog star Sirius, known as Sopdet, in the Egyptian language. It is also the last month of the Harvest season (Shemu). God willing and any day now the famous Nile inundation will begin. The appearance of Sirius rising in the eastern horizon (The Duat) just before dawn, warns us it's coming, although doesn't tell us exactly when.

So this is an ambiguous time, a twilight zone between the end of one long cycle and the beginning of another. From the time of the unification of Egypt in circa 3100BCE, the Egyptians had more or less abandoned their older lunar calendar in favor of this civil version. They retained the year of 360 days (12 months of 30days each duration). But now there are five additional days that lie in the limbo between one year and the next. It's likely that the Egyptians marked these days with special, propitiatory feasts or a fivefold communion.

Five particular gods get a "second" birthday here. In mythology the gods were expected to have two offspring, one male and one female. But famously Geb the earth god and Nuit sky goddess, break this pattern and have five children. It is for this very reason the "Heliopolitan" cosmology, refers to these five as the accursed generation. Is there a message there about ideal family size?

The Almanacs of Lucky and Unlucky Days tells us to

> "Make for thyself an amulet as protection, [drawn on fine linen] and placed about the neck (for the five) epagomenal days in (the name of) these gods on the day. . . written on the choice of. . . amulet. . .the female figure of Isis, the female figure of Nephthys . . . black colour anointed with first class oil and fumigated with incense on a burner, they should be purified, loosened, and thrown into water for the father Nun and for the mother Nut after the day of the birth of Ra and act. Behold, make for thyself a big Aabt-offerings of bread, beer, oxen, fowl, carob beans, incense, *ty-sps-wood* and all kinds of dates and vegetables — being clean, being clean in front of Ra Horakhty when he shines in the eastern horizon of heaven and when he sets in the western horizon. Behold, thou bathest in the fresh water ... of the beginning of inundation. Paint thine eyes with green paint; take a drink of wine and anoint thyself..."

The great ones are born. As for the great ones whose forms are not mysterious, beware of them. Their occasion (or, deed) will not come. They have proceeded.
Birth of OsirisOsiris,
Birth of Haroeris (Horus the Elder),
Birth of Set,
Birth of Isis,
Birth of Nephthys.
As to anyone who knows the name of the five epagomenal days, he does not hunger, he does not thirst, Bastet does not overpower him. He will not enter into the great law court, he will not die through an enemy of the king and will not die (or, depart) through the pestilence of the year. But he will last every day (till) death arrives, whereas no illness will take possession of him.
As to him who knows them, Hu/HwHu/Hw will be prosperous within him, his speech is important to listen to in the presence of Ra.
There are special prayers for each day, for example :
Third day : the birth of Set. Words to be said on it:
"Oh, Set, Son of Nut, great of strength, save me from bad and evil things and from any slaughter, protection is at thy hands of thy holiness. I am the son of thy son."
The name of the day: "It is powerful of heart."
And words to be said when the epagomenal days are completed.
"Hail to you! O great ones according to their names, children of a goddess who have come forth from the sacred womb, lords because of their father, goddesses because of their mother, without knowing the necropolis. Behold, may you protect (me) and save me. May you make me prosperous, may you make protection, may you repeat and may you protect me. I am one who is on their list."
This spell is to be said four times.

So there's plenty of magical work to be done. I use the summer solstice as the calibration point in my own lunar calendar (see links on www.ombos.co.uk) for current data. I will be at Stonehenge for the solstice eve, observing the rising of the stars, which I'd suggest is part of its original function.

July . . . Thoth

By convention the first month of the Egyptian year was named after and sacred to the god Thoth. Thoth has two major forms either as a baboon or the Sacred Ibis. Khonsu is an androgynous moon god like Horus or Set the "Left Eye of Ra" and "Ra in the underworld or Duat". Thoth's birth as the moon is related in the so-called homosexual episode in *The Contendings of Horus & Seth* (reproduced in *The Bull of Ombos*). Although Set is male, he is able to give birth to Thoth. In fact many of the Egyptian gods have male and female qualities, including the sun god Ra!

As the god of scribes and by extension magicians, by late Egyptian times, every utterance Thoth's made was considered magical. Although Ptah is said to have devised the original hieroglyphs, it is Thoth who simplified them into two dozen basic signs used by the scribes. Thus he could be said to be the creator of the alphabet. Thoth's presentation of the core or seed of the alphabet drawn from the mysterious primary forms, is the basis of Hermeticism, the magical tradition that bears his name in Greek translation.

New Year's day falls in his month. The name of the month is another reminder of Egyptians lunar calendar (see later chapters). This month is also a celebration and propitiation for a dangerous time between the years. I guess also because the calendar, whether lunar or solar requires certain "arcane" calculations of the kind discussed later, this kind of activity might be considered Thoth's domain.

Thoth was exalted on the 19th day of this month. The 19th day of July has no particular significance in our own calendar nor indeed the Egyptian civil year. If it was the nineteenth day of the lunar cycle, the moon would be past full but still in its "white night" period (see below). As we shall see, the birthday of most of Egypt's gods and goddesses is celebrated on the full moon day. Why should Thoth's birthday follow a different rationale? We will probably never know for certain. The Egyptologist Anthony Spalinger[10] has an ingenuous theory that 19 is the difference between 365 (the solar year) and 384 (the lunar year) ie -11 (or +19). For me there may be some additional reason. My own suggestion, which seems not more convoluted that Spalinger, is that 19 years is sometime to do with the complete lunar cycle as discovered by the Babylonian astronomers. A lunar calendar needs 19 years to complete the cycle. The 19 years consist of 12 years with 12 new moons and 7 years with 13 new moons. In so many ways, Thoth is a moon god whose significance survives the changeover from lunar to solar calendar and can be considered the deity of the entire year..

August . . . Answer my question

The second month of the inundation featured the most famous of all Egyptian holy days - the 'beautiful Feast of Opet'. There was a procession during which Amun of Karnak journeyed southward to the temple of his consort Mut at Luxor. Amun/Amun-Ra is the Egyptian national flag carrier. A special sacred road connected both of these great temples. However in later times both journeys were made by river. Crowds of pilgrims towing the god's ceremonial barque assisted the outward one against the stream. These strenuous activities were lightened by drinking songs whose origin is very ancient.

The melee was also an occasion for oracular appeals to the god. The Egyptian temple cult was very elitist and the majority of ordinary folk were excluded. However the consultation of omens and oracles was for everyone and became so popular that over time it changed Egyptian religious practice bringing personal interaction with the gods and spirits. During this festival priests carried the portable images of the gods out of their seclusion on special barque shrines. Anyone in the vast crowd could now come before this moving shrine and pose a direct yes/no question to the god. The answer was determined by whether the priests carrying the shrine made a step backwards or forwards - forward for yes, backward for no. Yes there is scope for manipulation of the result but also, given the swirling ecstatic mass of people, there is also opportunity for the god to reply directly through random chance. In a later chapter I present other kinds of common folk omens including the many lunar observations.

What happens when Amun reached Luxor is the subject of a great deal of speculation, especially concerning the role of a priestess called 'God's Wife.' Possibilities include some form of sacred marriage involving sexual rites in the so-called 'birth room', in which the divine king was conceived by Amun.[15]

The feast began on the *evening* before the 15th day of second civil month of Akhet and continued for pretty much the rest of the month. The 15th day is the full moon, thus it is reasonable to suppose this was originally a full moon feast, that continued for the remainder of the lunar fortnight. There are no records of this feast before the 18th Dynasty, but by the reign of queen Hatshepsut it was an annual event. It survived until the fall of paganism, with echoes in subsequent Coptic Egypt.

September . . . The world oldest myth?
There is a very ancient and sustained connection between this month and the goddess Hathor. Hathor's story begins somewhere in the mists of time as an ancient neolithic cattle goddess. This talk of blood reminds me of what is said to be the world's oldest myth "The Destruction of Humanity" as related in "The Book of the Heavenly Cow".

The myth tells of a rebellion of humanity against the aged sun god and demiurge Ra. As punishment Ra sends his fiery eye personified as Hathor, to cull the "divine cattle". The "divine cattle" is an euphemism for humans beings. In a later version it is the fiery lion goddess Sekhmet who does the deed. All Egyptian gods are fond of blood and Hathor is no exception. She enjoys the task so much that like the goddess Kali, she becomes mad with blood lust and the "cull" threatens to become genocide.

Ra distracts her with another favourite tipple of the gods, the ancient sacrament of beer laced with red ochre, which tastes like blood. This myth perhaps marks the moment at which beer is substituted for blood as a key offering in religious rites.

Hathor's inner nature reminds me a lot of another archaic stellar deity called Set. Is it possible they were once connected - I think so? They both share a love of sex, music, dance and drunkenness. So much so that the phrase "All acts of love and pleasure are her rituals" seems to fit like a glove.

From the day of one's birth Hathor records one's fate in her book. When one's time is up she sends her seven demonic emissaries (the *Hatayou*), armed with flint knives, to "cut the flowers". The task of the magician is to remove names from her book and thus cheat or manipulate fate, but that's another story.

In later times the most prominent festival associated with Hathor was her sacred marriage as Mistress of Dendera to Horus of Edfu. Coming as it does towards the end of the season of inundation, the river is more navigable and Hathor's month involves a great deal of activity on the river. Her cult statue was taken by boat to Edfu, arriving on the new moon and lingering 13 days until just before the full moon.

October . . . Osiris

If this corresponds to the Egyptian month Choiak then there is an indelible link with the cult of Osiris, the most famous of all Egyptian gods. In fact, half of all Egyptian religion revolves around the cult of Osiris, and the imperative to keep secret that which Set knows but threatens to reveal. The other half of Egyptian religion is about the sun god in his/her various guises, principally Amun-Ra.

The major festival of Osiris that falls in this month is clustered around the dark or waning half of the month on various days depending on which religious centre is studied.

The dead Osiris is the vanished moon. His day of embalmment is the day when the moon is never visible. But on the following day, Choiak 25, he shines forth from his temple at sunset, just as the crescent moon normally appears on the second day of the lunar month at sunset. If this be the resurrection of Osiris, which it certainly seems to be, since he wakes from his sleep and takes his place in the sky, then it is small wonder that Horus, son of Osiris, is born on the same lunar day on which his father is reborn.[18]

In my book *The Bull of Ombos* I present a text from a religious play, one of the oldest ritual dramas ever discovered, dating from the time of King Ramesses II (c1304-1237BCE). I've used sections of this as part of a contemporary pagan celebration of Lammas, which seems to have a great deal of common ground with the mythology of Osiris.

Abydos, an ancient religious settlement in Upper Egypt was the major cult centre of Osiris. The festival began with a procession of the jackal god Wepwawet (opener of the ways) from the temple. This was followed by the main procession in which the cult image of Osiris was carried by priests on a special barque. They circumambulated the temple walls before a vast crowd of pilgrims, no doubt accompanied by diverse ritual acts and dramas of a kind already mentioned.[17] See my book *Tankhem* for a discussion of these Mysteries in connection with the nearby Temple of Sety I.

The procession passes before an ancient terrace enabling the spirits of blessed dead to witness the divine theatre. The procession passes out into the desert to a place now known as Umm el-Qaab. This modern name means "mother of pots" a reference to the millions of small, offering pots littering the desert, the remains of many generations of pious offering. This is in fact a very ancient cemetery, in use from before the time of the earliest Egyptian Kings who are buried there in some style. Here at the legendary grave of Osiris, secret rites and Mysteries connected with his resurrection were performed. It is this secret rite that, according at least to the Osirian version of the myth cycle, Set the brother and murderer of Osiris "threatens" to reveal. This magical secret has exercised the mind of many subsequent practitioners who still seek to reveal it to their own initiates.

November . . . Samhain & the "Wheel of the Year"

A fellow Companion of Set asked me – "Tell me again, when is Set's birthday? Never mind all the complex stuff, just tell me the bottom line." I narrow it down to two options – one for those who want to return to the Lunar-Sothic calendar and make the observation in the same manner as our Egyptian ancestors did circa 3500BCE. The other is to use the epagomenal or extra days. For it was once said that five important gods were born on each of those days: Osiris, Horus the Elder, Set, Isis and Nephthys.

Set's birthday is the third epagomenal day, but when would that be?

Lunar Sothic calendar. We are currently in fourth year of the nineteen-year lunar cycle. By my calculation the new lunar year began on 22nd June 2009. This year has an extra lunar month known as "Thoth" by the very ancient Egyptians. (Contemporary European pagans know this intercalary month as "Ice moon"). The lunar month is "Tekh" meaning "the cup" (of intoxication) started on 22nd July 2009. This month is sacred to Sethians, therefore we decided to celebrate Set's birthday on the full moon or "white nights" around 7th August 2009.

If you prefer the late Egyptian Solar calendar, then one solution might be to pay attention to the 31st day of the month *in order* from the new-year, nominally July. This would make Seth's birthday 31st October – celebrated as Samhain in neo-paganism and strangely appropriate.

Before the building of the Aswan High Dam, the Nile's flood would be receding and the fields would again be available for cultivation. The literal meaning of the month name is "Swelling of the Wheat" – a reference to the quickening of the seed corn. And this is also the first month of "Peret", the season of winter. Peret is one of the three seasons of the Egyptian civil and ritual year – Akhet (Inundation); Peret (Winter) and Shemu (Harvest). The literal meaning of Peret is to go forth, presumably to walk on the fields and spread the seed. And, for understandable reasons, the Egyptians considered this almost as a second New Year.

The first day of this month then is special and set aside to a god that may be obscure but no less interesting for that. This is the time of "Nehebkau". Like many Egyptian gods, it can sometimes be difficult to decide whether he be god or demon. It's as well to remind ourselves that all Egyptian gods, like the elements, can have their unpleasant side. Nehebkau is a serpent divinity with an alarming resemblance to that most chaotic of entities, Apophis – demon of non-being. The colossal, female serpent Apophis or Apep is the nearest the Ancient Egyptians ever got to absolute evil.

Nehebkau, whose name means 'bestower of dignities' – was perhaps once a dark brother of Apophis. Unlike Apophis, Nehebkau, one time enemy of the sun god Ra, is somehow brought on side. Some experts think Nehebkau was connected with the original and very ancient Egyptian lunar calendar. And this entire month was once dedicated and indeed named after the powerful serpent demon. Like many Egyptian ritual days, honoring Nehebkau should best be done on the new or full moon.

If you want some words, then I can offer just a few clues from Egypt's terse Pyramid Texts. It comes from a section when the deceased is ascending to heavenly rebirth.

> Greetings to thee, O Horus, in the regions of Horus;
> Greetings to thee, O Set, in the regions of Set;
> . . .
> Greetings to you, ye two harmonious (goddesses),
> daughters of the four gods,
> who dwell in the great palace (Heliopolis),
> Come forth and hear my voice,

> Let me see you as you really are.
> Let me look upon you:
> As Horus looked at Isis
> As Nehebkau looked at Selket, the scorpion goddess
> As Sobek, the crocodile looked at Neith,
> the ancient Mother Goddess
> As Set looked to the two harmonious (goddesses).
> (Pyramid Text, Utterance 308, Translated by Mercer).

From which we learn that Nehebkau had a mother, the scorpion goddess Selket. Time then to welcome the old forgotten ones in from the cold. They may have some special secrets to enable us to remove the sting or some of the other poisons from our life.

No one has yet discovered a full account of the story of how this powerful demon came again to live with humans. His serpent image often decorates the throne of the goddesses Sekhmet and Bastet. To fight a demon, you need a demon. It is said that the very ambiguous Egyptian god Set was created by the sun god Ra to deal with Apophis. Set spears Apophis and secures the progress of the sunboat for another day. Just as Set is powerful enough to deride Apophis, so the mighty lion headed Sekhmet is powerful enough to subdue Nehebkau. Thus Nehebkau adorns the throne of Sekhmet.

If Nehebkau shows up in your dreams and visions, could you ask him what transpired between he and Sekhmet in those forgotten times? Serpents - demonic and otherwise – crop up again in conjunction with the cult of the Decans, which is Egypt's proto-astrology. The Babylonians may have codified the Zodiac and passed this knowledge to the Greeks, but when this knowledge arrived in Egypt, it's likely that the priests said they had their own equivalent of the Zodiacs from time immortal. This is the system of 36 Decans, ten day or degree segments of the starry heavens. The combination of the (Egyptian) 36 Decans with the 12 signs of the (Greco-Babylonian Zodiac) is the core of astrology ever since. The gods and goddesses of the Decans are lion headed serpents – there he is again – that Nehebkau, this time morphed into his mysterious partner lion-headed Sekhmet.

December . . . Dreaming

Last night I dreamt I was standing on the threshold of the Holy of Holies of an Egyptian temple. My task there was to look after the rather splendid robe for the High Priest or was it the god? Which is maybe a reminder that this, the second month of the Ancient Egyptian winter (Peret) was a time when the Ancient Egyptians looked after their clothing and gathered around bonfires in the fields for the celebration of various new moon fire festivals.

Our Egyptian ancestors gave various names to this month. If one follows the later Civil calendar, then it is "Mechir" – Feast of Clothing although its older name was "Rekh Wer" – The Great Fire Festival. Also in this month, perhaps on the new moon, could be placed a festival of Anubis. The "clothing" could be wrapped up in the process of mummification that the jackal headed one supervises.

Any lunar calendar needs some form of calibration to keep it in synch with the seasons; remembering that each solar year can have 12 or 13 lunations. In other words, every third year will require an extra, thirteenth month. And the decision on when to add this extra month will be governed by an observation of the sky – either connected with the solstice or with the rising of the Dog Star Sirius. Thus very Ancient Egypt had two lunar calendars - Lunar-Solar and Lunar Sothic versions.

The Lunar-Solar version was popular in Egypt's Nile delta region. Observations to calibrate this no doubt involved the point at which the sun breaks over the horizon at dawn on the solstice. At the summer solstice, the sun is at its most northerly rising point. In Egypt this will be north-eastern N65°E. Over the coming days and months it makes the journey 'south' to its most southerly rising point at the winter solstice north-eastern N118°E. Winter or summer solstice would provide suitable fixed points at which to decide whether an extra lunar month is required – the formula based on how many days the old moon has left to run when the solstice occurs. It's the kind of calculation any modern pagan and indeed the average Ancient Egyptians could make.

A number of Egyptian temples have winter sunrise orientations - one of the best examples is the temple of Hatshepsut at Deir el Bahri. Very few temples have summer solstice orientations. The sun god Ra's astrological journey is mirrored in Egyptian mythology. He is born at the winter solstice, and enters the underworld - the *duat* at the vernal equinox. During the hours of night he continues to travel and gestate there for the nine months (272 days) until, the following winter solstice, when he is again reborn. This mythology was underpinned by observations of the night sky, and especially the Milky Way, viewed as the body of the star goddess Nuit.

Richard Wells made the following interesting discovery:

> "It so happens that the outer arm of our galaxy, a band of myriads of stars called the Milky Way, when seen in its entirety over the course of a year has the appearance of a female shrouded in the thinnest of gauze robes. The Milky Way bifurcates into two appendages at the constellation of Cygnus forming the legs of the anthropomorphic body. Further along, the star clouds swell in the vicinity of Gemini to form the head with even the suggestion of the cloth headdress, hanging down the back." (Wells, RA (1994) 'Re and the Calendars' in Spalinger (1994) (ed.) in *Revolutions in Time: Studies in Ancient Egyptian Calendars*, Van Siclen, Texas.)

So Ra enters the *duat* at sunset on the spring equinox. In terms of the cycle of the year, this could be considered as the god's conception. If you were to look to that point in the west, an hour or two after sunset, when the sky is dark enough for you to see the Milky Way, you might observe an interesting phenomenon. The part of the Milky Way above identified as the head and especially the 'mouth' of Nuit, is over precisely the same spot. It is as if Nuit has just eaten the sun, which is in fact how this mystery is expressed in Egyptian mythology. The Birth of Ra occurs 272 days after conception, on the morning of the winter solstice. This period of gestation is the same for us lesser mortals. Rather amazingly the Birth of Ra also has a stellar component. The winter sun rises against a backdrop of the constellation Cygnus, whose star 'Y' corresponds with the 'yoni' or birth canal of Nuit!

With coincidences such as these, the solstice, the fire festivals and the lunar calendar, it's easy to see why modern pagans feel a strong affinity with their Ancient Egyptian ancestors.

1 The Archaic Lunar Calendar: Feasts, liturgy, prayers, hymns and spells

The very oldest Egyptian ritual calendar was lunar. The evidence for this is very complex and in the words of Professor Leo Depuydt, "does not exactly jump out at you!" This ancient lunar calendar continued a veiled existence alongside the dominant solar or civil year. In it we see a very ancient pantheon of gods, including Nuit, Min, & Hathor, one for each month of the lunar year. No doubt there were local variations, hence my own preference for Set in the first month. If this doesn't suit then I recommend making your own substitution, perhaps replacing Set with his offspring Thoth. Thoth presided over the "intercalary" month. As explained below, "intercalary" months were needed every three years to keep the lunar in synch with solar year. This then would be a year with a double helping of Thoth!

I have provided for them a unique collection of liturgy, ritual and prayers as may have been offered in the homes, sanctuaries and temples of the original Egypt.

Many of these feasts of Ancient Egypt were celebrated on the phases of the moon - principally when it was new or full. So whatever is your chosen favorite god or goddess, if you make your offerings on either of these days, you will be reviving the oldest and I'd say most authentic form of the ancient Egyptian magical religion.

So for example rites for the god Horus would fall in the moon's dark nights around the new moon; whereas those of his dark twin Seth occur on the full moon, the 'white nights' and especially the sixteenth day of the lunar month.

Inscriptions on Old Kingdom tombs (*mastabas*) tell us that the Egyptians observed ritual feasts at other phases of the moon.[1] Details on these celebrations are sketchy, but included the day of the moon's first visibility (*tep 3bed*). The heliacal rising of Sirius (*wep renpet* or *peret sepedet*) whose first appearance just before dawn heralded the season of Nile inundation was once used to calibrate the lunar calendar. There will be more to say about this in later chapters.

Timing for ritual

Ancient Egyptian liturgy was done thrice daily at approximately the third, sixth and ninth hour of the Egyptian clock. These times are standardised to 9am, 12midday and 3pm. The threefold execution reflects the traditional division of the sun into three phases as dawn, midday and sunset. (These times pass into Christian liturgy as *Terce*, *Sixt* and *None*.)

Rituals for thirteen lunar months

Table 1: Gods of Lunar Year					
Month	Neter	Name	Hieroglyphs	
(Jul)	Thoth	Thoth	*dhwty*	
1 (Jul-Aug)	Seth	Tekhy	*thy*	
2 (Aug - Sep)	Min	Phaophi	*p n jpt*	Akhet (inundation)
3 (Sep - Oct)	Hathor	Athyr	*Hwt-hr*	
4 (Oct-Nov)	Sokar	Choiak	*k3 hr k3*	
5 (Nov - Dec)	Neith	Tyby	*t3 ʿbt*	
6 (Dec - Jan)	Nuit	Mechir	*mhyr*	Peret (planting)
7 (Jan-Feb)	Anubis	Pharmenoth	*p n jmn htp*	
8 (Feb - Mar)	Renenutet	Pharmuthi	*p n rnwtt*	
9 (Mar - Apr)	Khonsu	Pachons	*Hnśw*	
10 (Apr - May)	Horus	Payni	*Hnt-hty*	Shemu (harvest)
11 (May - Jun)	Ipet	Epiphi	*ʿIpt*	
12 (Jun - Jul)	Ra Horakhti	Mesore	*mswt rʿ*	

Table 1: Months of the Lunar-Sothic Calendar

1st Month - Tekhy (July-August) Set

New Year's day was day one of the new lunar year (*tepy renpet*). This is an extra special new moon feast. The name of this month is Tekhy, which means literally 'the cup' hence a feast of drunkenness or intoxication. Alcohol was a big part of this, but also, the cup has additional associations with a psychoactive infusion made from the Blue Lily - as discussed in my book *Supernatural Assault in Ancient Egypt*. Although in later times this feast of drunkenness was associated with the goddess Hathor, it also seems to be very appropriate for the god Set whose existence is otherwise almost completely suppressed in later festival calendars.[2]

In my book *The Bull of Ombos*,[3] I discuss the controversial issue of whether Set could be the god sometimes referred to as 'The Elder Magician', i.e. as the first emanation of his father the Sun god Ra. Since writing, I have found further confirmation that 'The Elder Magician' has a defensive function guarding Ra from the Apophis. The Elder Magician is Set.[4]

Full Moon

As good a month as any to celebrate the ancient god Set. For this I suggest a rite entitled "The Stele of Jeu the Hieroglyphist". It uses a special "beneficial" sign or *sigil* known as a charaktêre as a focus. These signs are a specialised form of Egyptian Hieroglyph that developed at a time when the language was becoming part of a universal magical language still in use by practitioners. "Jeu the

Hieroglyphist" was a famous practitioner of his time; his name crops up in several places including in the magick of Gnostic Christians.

This ritual that has become important for occultists of the Thelemic tradition under the title "The Bornless One Rite" although we now know that "Headless" would be closer to the original sense. The ritual calls upon the services of a daemon known as the "Headless One" whom most Egyptologists say is a form of the god Seth. The "headless demon" is one of the many epithets of Seth and has numerous mythological and stellar meanings. In classical Paganism, there were thirty-six principal daimons, one for every ten day period, that which in astrology is known as a decan. These daemons are therefore the main influences of our personality and fate. One of the purposes of magick is to modify or even remove these conditions, enabling us to follow our own path. Thus "exorcism" can be viewed as a form of initiation.

Personally I find it useful when approaching new and complex ritual material to begin slowly by just sitting somewhere peaceful and reading the rite out. I may do this everyday over the course of a month, gradually working it all out before attempting a full "dramatic" performance, assuming that is the end in mind. I record dreams, memories and reflections in my lunar diary:

Sutekh of Hibis Oasis. Persian period image showing Sutekh or Seth subduing the "evil" serpent Apophis. This image thought by many scholars to be the prototype for St George and the Dragon.

<u>Preparation</u>: The original rubric suggests writing a formular on a new sheet of papyrus and wearing this as a headband. The magician faces north during the recitation. An alternative would be to draw with red pigment the special charaktêre on the forehead of those present. This charaktêre looks very much like the head of Set. Some of the words and chants may be unfamiliar thus as suggested elsewhere here is my mnemonic for the seven Greek vowels: FAther GEt GAme to FEEd the HOt NEw hÔme. These can be added in pencil next to each line where necessary.

Start with the *Tankhem* revised opening:
1. Hekas, Hekas, Este Babaloi
"Love and do what you will"

Face North and try to see the constellation *Ursa Major*. Draw down its power

Now turn to the East and say:
"Guardians of the House of Life at Ombos
Before me In the East: Nephthys
Behind me in the West Isis
On my right hand in the South is Set
And on my left hand, in the North Horus
For above me shines the body of Nuit
And below me extends the ground of Geb
And in my centre abideth the 'Great Hidden God' "

Make the "Horus Fighting" gesture.

[Breath in and in one perfect movement, form both hands into fists and raise them up and to the left of your head, stretch your right hand and arm in front of you and bring the left hand and arm to join it. As you finish the intonation, bring both hands back to the centre of your body]

Vibrate the first vowel long and hard - AAAAAAA -

Now turn to the North
Make the gesture "Horus Fighting" and vibrate the second vowel EEEEEEE, using the mnemonic gEt as above.

Then turn to the West
Make the "Horus Fighting" gesture and vibrate ÊÊÊÊÊÊÊ as in GAme

Turn to the South
Make the "Horus Fighting" gesture and vibrate IIIIIII as in fEEd

Return to face the East
Now bend over and reach out to the Earth
vibrating OOOOOOO as in HOt

Then gradually unfolding, come up and place your hands on your heart and vibrate YYYYYYY as in NEw

Finally stretching up to the heavens vibrate Ô Ô Ô Ô Ô Ô Ô as in HÔme.

Now make the sign of the (invoking) pentagramme in the air in front of you and vibrate
Aa, Eye, EE, Ou, Uh (Ay EAO - Oh Hail) Nephthys
Aa, Eye, EE, Ou, Uh (Ay EAO - Oh Hail) Horus
Aa, Eye, EE, Ou, Uh (Ay EAO - Oh Hail) Isis

Aa, Eye, EE, Ou, Uh (Ay EAO - Oh Hail) Set
Aa, Eye, EE, Ou, Uh (Ay EAO - Oh Hail) Geb
Aa, Eye, EE, Ou, Uh (Ay EAO - Oh Hail) Nuit
Aa, Eye, EE, Ou, Uh (Ay EAO - Oh Hail) Hidden God

Repeat first part that begins "Guardians of the House etc."
Return to the North

2. "I summon you, Headless One,
Who created earth and heaven,
Who created night and day,
You who created light and darkness;
You are Unas, the beautiful whom none has ever seen;
You are Iabas;
You are Iapos;
You have distinguished the just from the unjust;
You have made female and male;
You have revealed seed and fruits;
You have made men love each other
And hate each other."

"I am Moses your prophet to whom you have transmitted your mysteries celebrated by Israel; you have revealed the moist and the dry and all nourishment; hear me."

"I am the messenger of the beautiful Pharaoh Unas
This is your true name,
which has been transmitted to the prophets of Israel.
Hear me, Hear me,
ARBATHIAÔ REIBET ATHELEBERSÊTH [ARA]

BLATHA ALBEU EBENPHCHI CHITASGOê IBAÔTH IAÔ
Listen to me and turn away this daimon"

"I call upon you, awesome and invisible god with an *empty spirit*,
AROGOGO-ROBRAÔ

SEKHMET

MODORIÔ PHALARCHAÔ OOO

Holy Headless One. Deliver us
From the daimon which restrains us,
ROUBRIAÔ MARI ÔDAM BAABNABAÔTH
ASS ADÔNAI APHNIAÔ
ithôlêth abrasas
AÊÔÔY;
Mighty Headless One,
Deliver us
From the daimons that restrain.
MARARRAIÔ IOêL KOTHA ATHORêBALO ABRAÔTH,

Deliver us:
AÔTH ABRAÔTH BASYM ISAK SABAÔTH IAÔ"

"He is lord of the gods;
He is the lord of the inhabited world;
He is the one whom the winds fear;
He is the one who made all things
By the commands of his voice."

"Lord, King, Master, Helper, save the Soul-*Ba* (Psyche)

ieou pyr

iou pyr

iaôt

iaêô

ioou

ABRASAX SABRIAM

OO YY EY OO YY

ADÔNAIE,

Immediately, immediately
Good messenger of the God
ANLALA LAI GAIA

APA DIACHANNA CHORYN"

Assumption of the God form

"I am the headless daimon with my sight in my feet;
[I am] the mighty one [who possesses] the immortal fire;
I am the truth who hates the fact that unjust deeds
are done in the world;
I am the one who makes the lightning flash and the thunder roll;
I am the one whose sweat is the heavy rain, which falls upon the
earth that it might be inseminated;
I am the one whose mouth burns completely;
I am the one who begets and destroys;
I am the Favour of the Aion;
My name is a heart encircled by a serpent;
Come forth and follow."

"Subject to me all daimons,

So that every daimon,
Whether of the heavens
Or the air
Or earthly
Or under the earth
Terrestrial or aquatic,
Might be obedient to me
And every enchantment and scourge
Which is from God."

Closure:
When you want to finish do so by for example repeating the first part of Tankhem opening and then a "license to depart":
"I release any spirits entrapped by this working,
May you go in peace to your lovely abodes.
Farewell Headless One,
Lord of the inhabited world,
Farewell Akephalos,
The son of Nuit
Leader of the company of heaven in their diurnal motion,
Senebty, great Bull of Ombos."

After which pour any remaining offerings such as those of the chalice on earth and clear equipment, extinguish lamps etc .[9]

Notes & Sources

I've used some "poetic licence" with the text which is mainly from PGM V 96-172 translated D E Aune and published Betz, H D (1986). Betz cites Reiling, J "Hermas and Christian Prophesy" NT.S 37 (Leiden Brill 1973) 41-48 as an informant on Pagan technical term "empty spirit" but I didn't find him that revealing on the Pagan usage and was really an apologia for the Christian use of same. This ritual is translated (in German) and discussed in *Abrasax II* Merkelbach & Totti pp 153-70. They also concur that the "headless" god combines elements of several gods, principally Set. I've rendered the god name "Osor-Onnophris" (Egyptian *Wsir Wn-nfr*) as "Unas the Beautiful" rather than "Osiris, the beautiful being". Aleister Crowley, in his celebrated version of the rite also "suppresses" the name *Osiris*, rendering it as "Myself made perfect". My intuition is that Pharaoh *Unas* of the fifth dynasty fits here. He was one of the builders of the great pyramids with their innovative magical texts. There are other interesting coincidences between Unas and this text. It's the only substantive change I've made. I've not followed Crowley versions of the god names, e.g.: he substitutes "Ankh ef n Khonsu" for "Moses"; who at the time of the rite's composition was regarded in Egypt as an important magician.

2nd Month (August-September) Min

Celebrations of Min's birthday are recorded on Egypt's oldest memorials such as the 1st Dynasty Palermo stone. But his cult is even older reaching back to the prehistoric era when he was a deity of fertility, sexual reproduction and natural phenomenon such as storms. His erection is his most famous attribute – combined as it is with his raised arm and flail some have speculated that this is all part of an aggressive/protective posture?

His main centres were Koptos (Kuft) & Panopolis (Akhmim). His symbols are the Thunderbolt, the White Bull, the Flail and the Phallus. Wallis Budge speculates there was also a lunar component to his cult. Min is also called *ka-mwt-f* "Bull of his mother" a reference to the incestuous impregnation of his mother, an epithet of various gods, including Horus, also Geb who kills his father Shu in order to ravage Tefnut. Before getting too outraged, it's as well to remember this is an agricultural motif and refers to reproductive activity of bulls and cows. Min's archaic shrine was a phallic shaped hut, woven from two significant and emblematic plants – the White Lotus & the (narcotic) Blue Lily (*Nymphaea caerulea*)

The blossoms and foliage of these flowers are to be woven into model phallus or perhaps crown. The traditional hymns are referred to as "Danced", implying they are rhythmic chants.

Min from The Temple of Hibis in El Khargeh Oasis (see Winlock, et al 1941-154). The god's phallus mutilated in late classical period, probably as an act of counter magick. The worshipper is shown offering Min lettuce, his preferred food.

Danced Hymn for Min who is on his staircase

Hail to you,
Min, Min Ra
Welcome
On your staircase

Hail to you
Min, Min Ra
And the crown you wear
on your forehead

Hail to you
Mysterious Min
"Bull of his mother"
Much that you do remains in obscurity

You are unique
To whom praise is given
You have power to give life
To those you love

Powerful to give him to be propitiated
He is unique here
To whom has been conferred the function
of the unknown god

While you go out of the great door
And are standing on your stairway of truth
Speaking with Osiris hour by hour

See, that which you ordain
For protection
Against all bad things
Min justified before your enemies

In the sky and on the earth
By the judges of all the gods
And all the goddesses.

Hymn to Min as the Sickle (Kapesh)
[To be performed whilst offering a sheath of wheat to Min as White Bull)

Prophets of Min
We carry his sceptre and crown
The town of Buto does not push us back
Seizing your white & red crown
The servitors of Horus & Set
Are at peace in Thebes & Coptos
Those of the bee [are at peace]
The Prophets of Min [are at peace]
The Dancers of Min [are at peace]
The people of Gold [are with us/me]
The northern place, of Pe [are with us/me]
The southern place, the Ape of Thoth [are with us/me]
And place of Natron [are with us/me]
The image of Min approaches its resting place
Mother Isis brings the danced hymn
Which comes out of her mouth,

The goddess and sister of his home town (Koptos)
Min be strong and powerful for us/me
Min be victorious over our/my enemies

Valediction:
I give you the panegyric of Ra
I give you courage and strength

Notes & Sources
Danced hymns translated by Henry Gauthier and published in his *Les fêtes du dieu Min*, Cairo 1931, pages 231 & 241. J R Ogdon "Some notes on Iconography of Min" in *Bulletin of the Egyptology Seminar [of New York]* vol 7 (1985-86) pp.29-41 - theorizes that characteristic posture of Min is not about fertility but a threatening gesture i.e. guardianship. This same gesture is used in the Tankhem Opening, itself based on classical Pagan sources. Easler, A N "Raised Arm Figures & the Iconography of the Egyptian God Min" *Bulletin of the Egyptology Seminar [of New York]* vol XI pp.109-118. Easler opines that Min's "thunderbolt" is more likely the hieroglyphic sign for "doorbolt" - a quintessentially protective object, the focus of an important act of magick in several other contexts. For old liturgical hymn of 12th Dynasty see H O Lange, *Das Weisheitsbuch (Wisdom Book) des Amenemope*, Kopenhagen 1925; Budge, E A Wallis (1904) *The Gods of the Egyptians,* London. Grimm, A (1994) *Die ältägyptischer Festkalender in den Tempein der Griechisch Römischen Epoche*, Wiesbaden/Harrassowitz, discussion of Parker's Ptolemaic evidence concerning the feast of Min (see Parker 47-50 §238-51)

 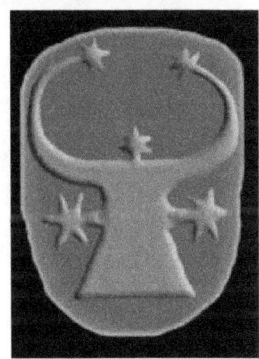

Top: Pectoral ornament, Horus and Set worshipping Bat, an archaic goddess later assimilated to Hathor. Middle Kingdom, 12th Dynasty, probably reign of Senworsret II or III, 1898-1841BC, probably from Dahshur. Electrum with remains of lapis lazuli, carnelian and feldspar inlays, Height 1.5 ins. Myers colections, Eton College. Published in Spurr, Stephen, *Egyptian Art at Eton College* : New York, N.Y. : Metropolitan Museum of Art; Windsor: Eton College, c1999. Bottom *Left*: image of Bat from 1st Dynasty Narmer Palette, *Right*: The predynastic "Hathor Palette" showing Bat as celestial cow - Petrie (1953) *Ceremonial Slate Palettes*.

Hathor from Tomb of Sety I, From I Rosellini (1832-44)
Monumenti dell' Egitto e della Nubia, Pisa.

Month III (September - October) Hathor

Although the goddess Hathor is known as the bestower of human fertility, there are traces that this quality extents to animals and indeed crops. The myth of "Seth & the Seed goddess" concerns *seed* in all its connotation including semen and the female equivalent. The following dedication is adapted from traditional spells of the time of King Rameses II.

Why this is so (this part of the spell is to be read out)
Once upon a time
The Seed Goddess Hathor (*t3 mtwt*)
Took a bath on the shore in order to purify herself in the oasis
Seth was out walking and he saw her
He saw her jewel encrusted girdle, he saw her bare ass,
And it turned him on
Then he mounted her as a ram mounts a ewe
He covered her as a bull covers a cow
But for the seed goddess it was all wrong
And she went straight to his head
To the region between his eyebrows where the full moon sits
And he lay down, exhausted on his bed
and was stricken with the seed become poison
Then his other wife Nephthys (Anath),
The victorious goddess
An androgynous woman who acts like a warrior
Who wears a man's kilt
Tied with a woman's sash

Distressed, went to her father the Sun god Ra
He said "what is the matter with you"
Nephthys, victorious goddess
Androgynous woman who acts like a warrior
Who wears a man's kilt
Tied with a woman's sash
I am near to my evening setting
I know you want me to cure Set of the effects of his overstrenous coupling with Hathor
The poison of the bad seed out of place
Let Set's stupidity be a lesson for him
Hathor, the seed goddess was destined for the bed of the sun god above
He will make love to her with his heavenly fire
His will be as hard as steel when he enters her.

Hearing this the divine Isis said:
I am the Nubian woman
I have come down from heaven
I have come to realise the seed in the body
of every mother's son and every mother's daughter
And cause them to return in good health
For as Horus lives
So shall all live:

2. The lunar blessing:
1. I place Hekayet in my forehead
So no bad thing shall take its stand in there

2. I place Horus Mekhantenirti in my eyes
So no bad thing shall take its stand there

3. I place Khenem-tjaw of Hesret (Breeze-sniffer) in my nose
Beware lest she extinguish the north wind in the presence of the great ones

4. I place Anubis in my lips
So no bad things will take its stand there

5. I place Sefekh-'abui in my tongue
So no bad things will take its stand there

6. I place Buto in my neck

7. I place the voice goddess Meret in my throat
Beware lest her voice be lacking in the presence of Ra

8. I place Nut in my nipples
The lady who bore the gods and gives them suck

9. I place Montu lord of both arms
So no bad thing will take its stand there

10. I place Ra Lord of the vertibrae
So no bad thing will take its stand there

11. I place Set lord of the side
So no bad thing will take its stand there

12. I place the four sons of Horus in my liver, lung, heart and kidneys, spleen, intestines, ribs and flesh
So no bad thing will take its stand there

13. I place Hathor in my flank
So no bad thing will take its stand there

14. I place Horus in my phallus
So no bad thing will take its stand there

15. I place Reshpu in my bone marrow
So no bad thing will take its stand there

16. I place Horus in my thighs
So no bad thing will take its stand there

17. I place Sia (wisdom) in my knees
So no bad thing will take its stand there

18. I place Nefertem in my shin
So no bad thing will take its stand there

19. I place Nebet Debwet, Lady of the soles of my feet
So no bad thing will take its stand there

20. I place Anukis in my toe nails
So no bad thing will take its stand there

21. I place Serket, lady of the bite
So no bad thing will take its stand there

Notes & Sources

Gardiner (1935) *Hieratic Papyri in the British Museum 3rd Series* p 61-65 spell Vs I 4-6, 7; Van Dijk, J (1986) " 'Anath, Seth and the Seed of Ra" in Hospers, J H, *Scripta Sigma Vocis*, Gronigen; Pinch, G (1993) *Votive Offerings to Hathor,* Oxford; Roberts, A (1995) *Hathor Rising, The Serpent Power of Ancient Egypt,* Northgate

THE RITUAL YEAR IN ANCIENT EGYPT

Image (detail above) of the Boat of Sokar from a table with the name of Egypt's first pharaoh, Menes. Restored and reproduced in Allan Gardiner (1961) *Egypt of the Pharaohs*, OUP.

Image of Sokar from Tomb of Sety I, From I Rosellini (1832-44) *Monumenti dell' Egitto e della Nubia*, Pisa.

4th Month (October-November) Sokar

Sokar is a more primitive version of his well known successor Osiris. He is an archaic god of the underworld and the necropolis. He is depicted as a mummiform god with a hawk's head. He is associated with kingship but also agriculture and rituals of water. His rites began as "sabbatic" rather than annual celebrations; inscriptions talk of a festival every six years. These rites involved hoeing or breaking the earth, probably as a symbolic beginning of the winter sowing; also circumambulation around the boundaries of cities, buildings, temples and tombs not unlike the rite known in some parts of Europe as "beating the bounds". Celebrants wore necklaces woven of vegetables - usually onions or garlic. It was also a time to offer vegetables to the dead.

The focus of cult acts was a distinctive ritual boat – that of Maarty (double Maat). For the following rite I draw an image of this boat on the earth in cornflower rather like a Voodoo Veve or Hindu mandala. The participants – "Prophet" (priest) and a congregation representing the seven "Hathors" arrayed around the image.

The priest begins with the following "voice offering".

To Sokar: In his shrine called Shetayet
To Sokar: In the house
To Sokar: In centre of the temple (Hry Ib)
To Sokar: In the necropolis
To Sokar: Upon the distant hills
To Sokar: Presiding one in the tent of the craftsmen

To Sokar: In many places and lands
To Sokar: In the boat of double Maarty
To Sokar: In Egypt
To Sokar: And in foreign lands
To Sokar: In the southern and northern lakes
To Sokar: In heaven, on earth and in all his temples
To Sokar: In all of his places, shrines and tombs
To Sokar: In every place he likes to be
To Sokar: In all his images
To Sokar: We celebrate your festival, eternally
To Sokar: We walk the boundaries and beat the earth.

Litany of Sokar
Hail: Be triumphant O Sovereign
Hail: How sweet is the fragrance that you love
Hail: Behold, I perfume the things you love
Hail: I shall do what you please
Hail: I kiss the earth; I open the way with libation
Hail: Oh favoured one of Abydos
Hail: Fiery of eye, son of a prophet
Hail: I make protection according to what you say
Hail: I love your face when you rest in the god's broad hall within the temple
Hail: Abydos has for name Abydos
Hail: Abydos has for name Abydos
Hail: How pleasant is the fragrance of Abydos
Hail: Abydos is doubly protected
Hail: My God, hearken to this rite
Hail: Pray be joyous and hearken thou to the worship that comes from the mouth of Egypt

Hail: As for a servant who follows his lord,
Bastet shall not have power over them

Hail: Please drive away our enemies

Hail: Please come and instruct the young

Hail: Put the fear of you into the chaotic

Hail: Be thou seated and come thou, O weary hearted one

Hail: The son of a prophet it is who recites this ritual

Hail: Enduring of name in Djedu

Hail: Secret fragrance of Djedu

Hail: May you live forever

Hail: Your festivals shall be everlasting

Hail: The Lord of Djedu has come

Hail: He has smitten our enemies

Hail: For the good god beloved of Sokar

Hail: He may grant very many returns to us

The rubrik says to be recited sixteen times but I found once was enough. I've used this ritual with a small group and saw possibilities to include the Egyptian "call and response" componant in any future performance.

Hathor's can also say:
"May she give life, stability and dominion
and all health to us like the sun god Ra forever".

Notes & Sources
Gaballa, G A and K A Kitchen "The Festival of Sokar", *Orientalia* 38 (1969) pp1-76 and plates. Allan Gardiner (1961) *Egypt of the Pharaohs* OUP.

Neith, showing her bow. Top right is her talismanic sign, two bows bound together. From J G Wilkinson, *Manners & Customs of the Ancient Egyptians*, 3 vols (Murray 1837)

5th Month (November - December) Neith

This month was often considered sacred to Min, whose festival was described earlier in connection with the second month. So rather than give Min a second bite of the cherry I've substituted some ritual material for an equally important deity Neith, one of Egypt's oldest goddesses. Some say she was one of the consorts of Set, and that it is her arrow that protrudes from his flank; perhaps a message. Her forms are Cow, Beetle, Late Fish and Dwarf. Many of her attributes are set out in the hymns:

Hymn to the goddess Neith
To Adore Neith. Say:
1. You are the teacher of Sais
That is to say the earth (Tanen)
Among whom two thirds is masculine,
And a third feminine
Primal goddess mysterious and great,
Who was there at the beginning,
And inaugurates all things.

2. You are the celestial arch
In which the sun travels
The one who gives birth to the stars as long as they are,
And raises them on their portable shrines;
The breath which consumed the earth in the flame of her eyes,
The ardour taken out from her mouth;
The divine mother of Re, who shines on the horizon.
The mysterious one who shines with proper light.

3. You are the serpent goddess,
Manifested before all,
The protector of the entire land,
She who began to exist,
Before everyone else who has to be,
All who rule do so by her authority.

4. You are the one who made the lower World,
In its goddess form which reaches to
the borders of the universe,
In its material form as surface water,
In its name of "length without limit".
Mistress of the anointing oil
As well as rooms of cloth,
Goddess who divided the comb into five for its functioning
She who resides in the sky and the earth.

5. You are the expanse of water
Which made Earth (Tanen) and the primal waters (Nun),
And whom gave birth to everything that is;
(the one) who causes the inundation to flow in its time,
and the waters of renewal which gives a new life in its season;
(the one) who makes the vegetation sprout,
and creates the Tree of Life for living beings;
Raising the creative primal water (Nun)
Mehet-Weret, the Cow Goddess known as "the Great Flood"
Overcoming the one who rebels.

6. You are the mistress of Esna
Within the [mysterious] countryside
North of the [mound] of the two fledglings;
The one who nurses two crocodiles,
In their names Shu and Tefnut,
Guardian of their fortresses,
Who embraces the necks of two crocodiles
That is to say Re and Osiris
Both nestlings (children), sons of Re
in his chantry (Pi-Sahourê);
Who provides divine offertories for gods and goddesses.

7. Holy Cow.
Lady of southern place
The teacher of Re's country
In the middle of the [mound] of two nestlings;
Supporting the sky on your backbone,
Neith the great
Which gave birth to all beings,
And created grain [to nourish us]
Shu, son of Ra is maintained on your milk.
She nourished the "Seven Primordial Old Ones"
in the interior of the House of Gods
Rejuvenating Osiris lord of Life

8. You are the mistress of the brave
On the day of the fight,
You seize the bow and notch your arrow
Pushing back the hordes of rebels;

Overwhelming in her mightiness over the nine bows
The barbarians fall under your onslaught
Whosoever she favours will be king,
Horus, emblem of royalty eternally on their banners

9. You are the mistress of the sky,
Of the earth and the lower world,
Of the water and the mountains,
Your prestige everywhere elevated

10. You are the mistress of the palace
Protects the sovereign principal,
Maintaining its warriors,
And watching over the entire land
From the flood plain to the mountain top,
Great Uraeus serpent upon the forehead
of the gods and the goddesses,
Serpent of life that protects
And support benign governance
Through the body politic;
The Earth god revealing those worthy of support
So that the golden hawk
And humble lapwing are with her

11. Source of divine order
Ever watchful of intruders & impostors.
Kings depend on you for their power,

12. You are the mistress of the care-ers of the desert,
Lady of bracelets,
Teacher of travellers to the east,
Lady of Punt,
For whom the Fortress-of-the-Honeybee
is flooded with perfumes,
The smell of the cool olibanum,
Distilled drop by drop on curls on your hair
The white crown distinguishing your body
Gentle patroness of the living rock
Creatrix of every precious stone,
Of whatever purposes & function
You are venerated wheresoever they are mined
From Istéren to Rochet and Tefrer;
Lapis lazuli, turquoise and jasper.

Notes & Sources

El-Sayed, Ramadan (1975) *Documents relatifs à Said et ses divinités*, Cairo; El-Sayed, Ramadan (1982) *La Déesse Neith de Sais, Cairo;* Sauneron, S (1962) *Les fêtes religieuses d'Esna aux derniers siècles du paganisme*, Caire: Institut Français d'Archéologie Orientale.

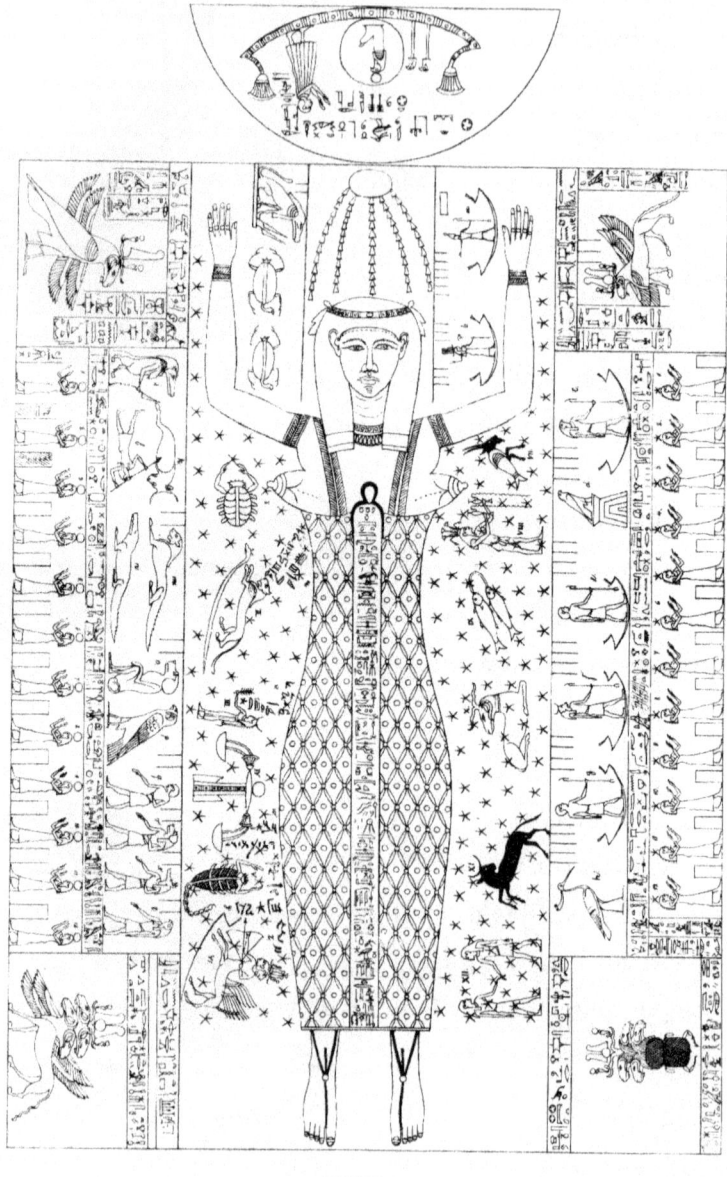

Nuit the star goddess, shown here surrounded by images of the planets, the four winds and the signs of the zodiac. Painting on inside of Heter's coffin, from Neugebauer O & Parker, R (1962) *Ancient Egyptian Astronomical Texts*, 4 vols, Brown University. Original now lost - Brugsch, *Recueil*

6th Month (December-January) Rekhwer (Greater fire festival)

For this month I'd suggest a celebration of the very ancient star goddess Nuit. For this I have adapted a dramatic text from the Osireion at Abydos. It comes from the *Book of Nut* or is more recent renaming as "The Book of the Fundamentals of the Stars". I have rendered the original in a more user friendly manner without changing the fundamental meaning which concerns the cycle of rebirth. The prayer is either done directly to Nuit or the Milky Way, or as a ritual for three or more participants, Nuit, the Star goddess; Shu the god of the Atmosphere and Geb the Earth:

The Dramatic Text in the Cenotaph of Seti I

Nuit:
"Stars that sail out at night
To the limits of the sky outside of my body;
Shine and be seen.
In the daytime you sail inside of me,
And are not seen.
Enter with the sun god Ra
And go forth after him.
Travelling with him on my body
Supported by Shu
Who settles you in your places (in the night sky)
When the sun god Ra sets in the western horizon.
My head is in the west
Enter my mouth
And I shall eat you!"

Geb:
"Sow who eats her piglets!" says earthy Geb quarrelling with Nuit, angry because she is always eating his children.

Shu:
"Let Geb beware! Says her father Shu, lifting her up, supporting her above himself, "Do not quarrel with Nuit for eating your children, for just as she gives birth to Ra everyday, so shall they live and go forth to their places from under her hind part in the East.
Not one of them has fallen since their birth.
The stars that go into the earth
Die and enter the Duat.
They stop in the house of Geb for seventy days.
Regenerated, loosing their impurity to the earth.
One does not speak the name of the one who is to be reborn,
During those seventy days.
For they have yet no identity
Until, as a shining star,
It rises at the end of the period of regeneration.
Nor do we name them among the 'living'
until all of its impurity falls to the earth
and like Sothis, it rises.
Then it is 'pure' (regenerated) and 'lives' again."

Nuit:
"The heads of gods are located in the east.
'one dies and another lives every ten days.'
They celebrate the First Feast, a birth day there."

"If their bones fall to the earth,
I give them back their head,
And their soul goes forth upon the earth."

"Tears fall and become as fish.
In a lake where the life of a star begins.
As a fish it grows and goes forth from the water.
From the sea it flies upward to the sky
From its former self it flies upward to the sky
From its former self rising as a star.
With other stars that go forth from the Duat
and withdraw across the sky."

Geb:

"I demand that the stars show their heads in the East!" Says Geb, prince of the Gods, again arguing with Nuit.
"Fish your own head out."

Thoth:

"Thoth commands it too, Fish out your own heads."

Nuit:

"Arise as stars I say, shining forth from the deep
Your burials like, those of men.
This period in the Duat just right for everything
That has to be done (for regeneration)."
"As souls you travel inside of the sky at night.
And then by day withdraw to the boundaries of the sky
Invisible to sight.

When seen by the living,
It is indeed as a star,
a piglet of your mother,
making its journey
and shining forth in the sky
in the hours of the night
Travelling the sky to the end."

"Thus all life is seen.
The stars go forth
outside of me, the goddess Nuit
Proceeding as they do and returning.
[The never-ending cycle of death and rebirth]
As the son succeeds the father
As new moon succeeds the full."

Notes & Sources

This ancient, and to many scholars, enigmatic drama is based on various sources, mainly Anne Sophie von Bomhard (2008) *The Noas of the Decades*, Oxford; Otto Neugebauer & Richard Parker (1960) *Egyptian Astronomical Texts*, London; Erik Hornung (1999) *The Ancient Egyptian Books of the Afterlife*, Cornell.

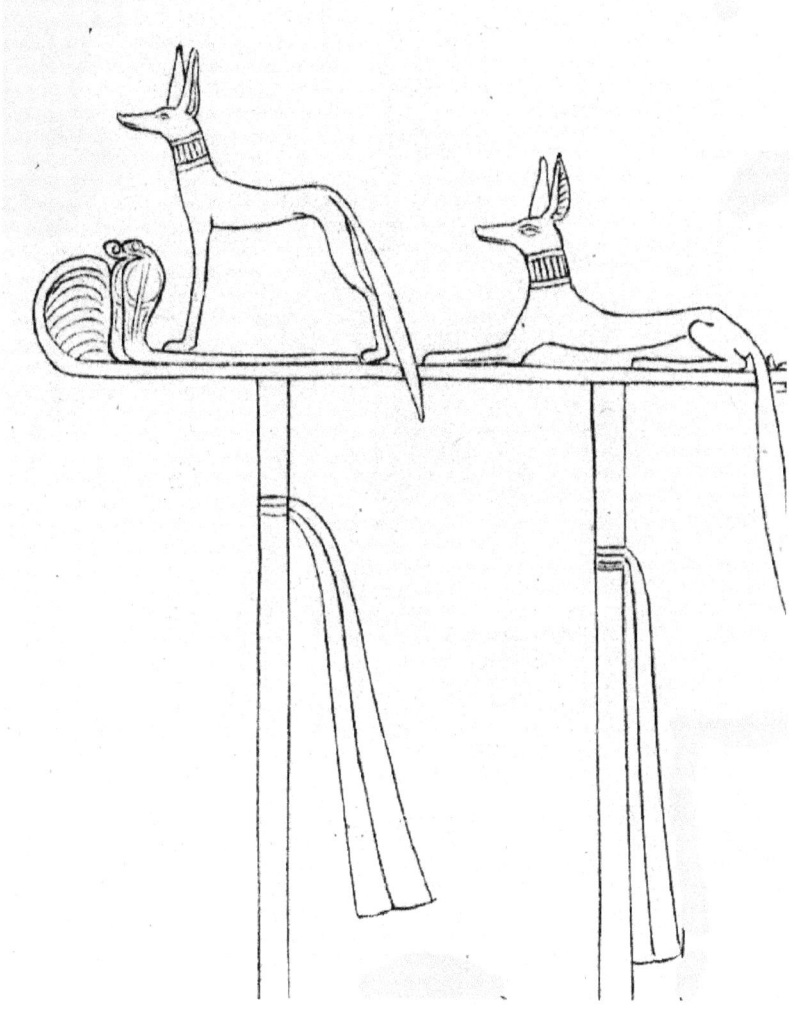

Ancient jackal deity Wepwawet/Upuaut 'Opener of the ways' from Temple of Sety I at Abydos drawn by Amice Calverley. His function was originally to open the field of battle.

Classic image of Anubis/Anpu, detail of painting from a private Theban tomb, From I Rosellini (Pisa 1832-44) *Monumenti dell' Egitto e della Nubia*

7th Month - (Jan-Feb)
(Lesser fire festival)
Wepwawet/Anubis

The Harris Magical papyrus (pHarris) show how there is a long association between the Jackal god Anubis and a technique known as a vessel divination or inquiry. His name, Egyptian *Inpw*, can mean child, which perhaps explains why these kinds of spell often stipulate that a youth acts as medium.

Anubis is most often said to be the child of Osiris & Nephthys. The spell uses various elements often associated with the god Set e.g.: oasis water and this may be because in for example the Papyrus Vandier the god Set is able to take on the form of Anubis. The spell is for general divine intelligence about the future. It aims to make contact with the divine spirits that control the "decans" i.e. fate as the astrological 'hours' at the time of the conjuration.

If the information you require is more specific then the ancients recommend submerging an *appropriate* object in the water or burning it on a brazier or thurible. So for example in the pHarris, the earliest known version of this spell, an "egg" of ass's dung is cast into water to repel bad influences.

The following spell is from one manuscript augmented with lines from related sources listed in the notes. If you check these sources I hope you will agree I have not distorted the original meaning merely interpreted and in some cases with the contemporary practitioner in mind, shortened the speeches. This kind of spell is often said to come from a physician in the *Oxyrhynchus* nome. Herm-Anubis is another important aspect of the god. For comments on the Sethian associations of Oxyrhynchus see *The Bull of Ombos*.

This rite is for two people, the priest who acts as amanuensis or scribe and a medium. It develops into a dialogue between the medium and the god Anubis. In classical times, the medium was usually a virginal youth but for this reconstruction I have it as a sensitive medium. For equipment one needs a suitable bowl or chalice into which one places clear water or oil, preferably from one of Egypt's oases. In addition a table altar on which to place food and drink as well as a thurible or brazier to burn incense and other magical catalysts. Egyptian magicians used a special Anubis herb for this rite. This has been variously identified as Stachys or Woundwort, which has a long medical history as a mild antiseptic and eye medicine. An alternative could be Mentha Aquatica/Water mint. It seems likely that the medium used an embrocation to open their inner eyes.

1. Start with the Tankhem opening as given earlier:

2. Priest: (opening address)
"Hail thou soul god, Anubis,
The son of the goddess Nephthys
Hail key-holder
Who sends the phantoms of the dead,
For my service in this very hour.
Hail Anubis loyal dog

Resting on a box of myrrh,
Your feet on the frankincense

When I make this libation
Anubis with a fair face
I see you great god
And with this masque (or mark) about my head
I am Anubis, master of secrets."

Priest:
"Oh Anubis, the edge of whose strap rests in Pelusium
Whose his face is like a spark
Put the light and breadth in my vessel
Open to me, O Earth!
Open to me, O Underworld!
Open to me, O primeval waters!
O protector of the necropolis at Abydos

Oh Gods who are in heaven
Who are exalted, come
And put the light and breadth in my vessel.

May we prosper for this vessel that was used by Isis
in her searching for Osiris
Powerful one of heaven, ABLANATHANALBA
The griffin of the shrine of the god who stands here today.

Then whisper:
"Oh good Oxherd Anubis,

My compeller, open the eyes of the medium so they may see.
O pure gods of the primeval water,
I am a child of earth by name,
Under the soles of whose feet the gods of Egypt are placed.
I am the one in the shrine
Of earth by name
I preserve the one in the shrine
With these forearms of real gold
The truth in my mouth is the honey of my lips.

Priest addressing the Medium:
"Open your [inner] eyes and tell me what you see?"

Medium:
[The following develops into a trance session. The text gives an idea of how this goes but in practice the participants would need to allow some flexibility. For example there needs to be a pause to allow the medium time to refocus and then whisper or otherwise signal they are beginning to see visions. They may say something like:]

"Be great, be great, oh Light"

Priest: (If necessary)
"Oh darkness, remove yourself from before him.
O light bring the light to me
Fate who is in the primal water
Bring the light into me
O Osiris who is in the divine bark

Bring the light in to me
O these four winds which are outside, bring the light in to me
O he in whose hand is the moment,
the one who belongs to these hours
Bring the light in to me
O Anubis, the good Oxherd, bring the light in to me
in order that you give me protection here today, for I am Horus,
the son of Isis, the good son of Osiris!
You should bring the gods for the place of judgement
and you should cause them to take care of my affair
so that my business proceeds
O those belonging to the avengers you should cause them
to do it for me"

Medium:
[They may repeat the simple sentence of before]:

"Be great, be great, oh Light".

Eventually they indicate when they can see Anubis
in their visions.

Priest:
Words before Anubis:
Oh RIDJ MYRIDJ,
Oh earth,
Great one of the earth
O this beautiful male whom Heset the daughter
of the Nemesis bore

Come to me, for you are this lotus flower, which came forth
from the lotus bud of Ra, which makes light for the entire land!

Hail, Anubis! Come to me!
O High one,
O mighty one O master of secrets for those in the Underworld
O Pharaoh of those in Amenti
O chief physician
O good son of Osiris
He whose face is strong among the gods
You should appear in the Underworld before the hand of Osiris
You should serve the souls of Abydos
In order that they all love through you
These souls, the ones of the sacred Underworld.
Come to the earth!
Reveal yourself to me here today
You are Thoth
You are the one, who went forth from the heart
of the great Agathodaimon,
The father of the fathers of the gods.
Come to the mouth of my vessel today
And tell me an answer in truth concerning everything
About which I am inquiring,
Without falsehood, therein, for I am Isis the wise,
the sayings of whose mouth come to pass.

[The original rubrik says repeat seven times which may be
excessive but perhaps one could apply to one small section as
this is an important symbolic instruction. Anubis then acts as

psycho pomp or mediator between the medium and the other gods and spirits.]

Priest: (speaking with a calm, slow voice)
"Ask Anubis to go forth and bring the gods in."

Medium:
"It is done" (or similar).

Priest (with calm, slow voice)
"Awaken to me,
Awaken to me Fate (Pshai)
Awaken Mera
The great one of the five (i.e. Thoth)
TSITSIY TENNDJIY
Do justice to me
Thoth, may creation fill the earth with light
O Ibis in his noble countenance,
Noble one who pleases the heart,
Create truth,
O great god whose name is great"

[The priest now focuses on the table set in order to entertain the gods. On the table is wine [or beer] and bread. This table is an altar but also the elaborate *mesa* as used in 'shamanism']

Priest to Medium
"Ask Anubis to bring in the gods to sit at the table".

Medium:
"It is done."

Priest to Medium
"Tell them it is open for the gods. Let them eat, let them drink, eat more, drink more, let them make merry."

Medium:
"It is done."

[The medium consults Anubis to ensure the divine guests are satisfied and for an appropriate moment to make the specific inquiry. When Anubis says the moment is come, ask Anubis to make the appropriate god stand up. When Anubis says the god has stood up, you say to Anubis to clear the table taking away that which is on it.]

Medium:
"Agathodaimon of today, lord of today, the one to whom these moments belong. Let him tell Anubis his name"

When he stands and tells his name you continue
asking every thing you wish.

"License to depart":
"Farewell, farewell Anubis the good Oxherd,
Anubis, Anubis, the son of a wolf and a dog
NABRIS-HOT HT [or *senebty*]
The cherub of Amenti

King of those of the Underworld" (repeat seven times)

After which pour the contents of the chalice on earth
And clear equipment, extinguish lamps etc.

Notes & Sources
This spell is based mainly on PDM xiv 1 - 92 with additional material from PDM xiv 425, PGM iv 1390-1495; PDM xiv 435sq, PDM xiv 2/7 in H D Betz (1986) *The Greek Magical Papyri in Translation*, Chicago; Jacques Vandier (1961) *Le Papyrus Jumilhac*, CNRS; The *Harris Magical Papyrus* is published in *Facsimiles of Egyptian Hieratic Papyri in the British Museum : with descriptions, translations, etc.* by E.A. Wallis Budge; British Museum, 1910, Col vii. This collection has several other interested ritual texts connected with Apep, Isis, Nephthys & Sokar. As an alternative to the use of a full Anubis mask, which can be troublesome if not well constructed, I suggest a small symbol of Anubis drawn on your forehead over the third eye or worn as a headband.

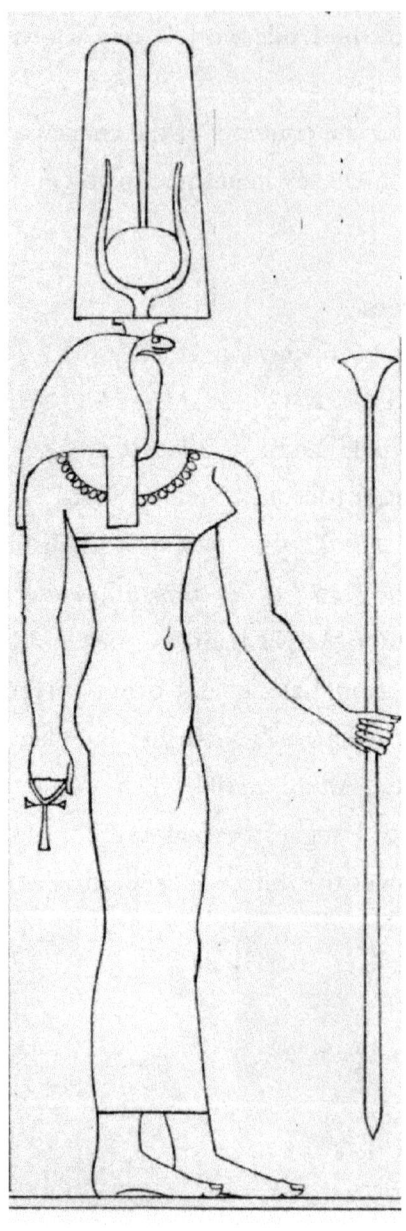

Image of Renenutet from Dendera, see Mariette-bey, Auguste (1870-1880) *Dendérah : description générale du grand temple de cette ville* / Vol III
PL75

8th Month (February – March) Renenutet (Greek Thermuthis)

Renenutet is an ancient serpent goddess associated with the harvest but also weaving and linen. Her usual form is that of a woman wearing the serpentine uraeus headdress, or a large snake wearing the solar disk and cow's horns. The association of snakes with harvested fields is perhaps a universal phenomenon, not to mention hazard that required some form of propitiation.

She is the mother of another mysterious serpent deity "Nehebkau". She may therefore share something with scorpion goddess Selket also said to be mother to Nehebkau. Both goddesses feed and nurture the future king. Selket is actually the non-venomous water scorpion, perhaps Renenutet is a non-venomous serpent.

Rubrik

Details of the cult practices are sketchy. It is probably an old harvest festival. One would expect a feast, possibly involving fire. This is also the birthday of the 'corn mummy' Neper. These are small dolls made of soil mixed with grain of corn, wrapped in linen and buried in the fields each year in association with the cult of Osiris.[32]

These rituals may be connected with marking out the fields at the beginning of harvest. There is perhaps some overlap with the Sed or 30 year jubilee rite of the king. Some say this 30 year interval is modeled on the 30 day lunar month. Among public rites, the chieftain is required to circumambulate the fields. *Encircling* was and indeed still is an important magical technique. This was no doubt modeled on the custom by which Egyptian folk circumambulated their fields in order to drive out the "pests of the year" – ie "pests" understood as physical and metaphysical entities.

Using these sources as clues I have compiled a short ritual for Renenutet. This could be combined with the construction of a small "corn-mummy" to be buried in the ground at the rite's conclusion.

1. The *Tankhem* / Heptagram opening given earlier is here especially relevant. The version I use is from the Greco-Egyptian magical papyri but others found in records for the Sed rituals (see Uphill in *Notes & Sources*) echo the same geomantic principles.

2. "I take my stand on the staircase of the south
on the festival of Renenutet"

The Abydos Formula
"Before me in the east is Nephthys
Behind me in the west Isis
On my left hand in the south is Horus
And on my right hand in the north is Set
For above me shines the body of Nuit
And below me extends the ground of Geb
And in the centre abideth the 'Great Hidden God.'
Then to each direction say:

" 'To the ground' I say as Hekaw the Elder magician"

3. How beautiful is Sobek,
He of Crocodile city, (namely) Horus,
The one who is in the midst of Shedyet (Crocodile city)
Who appears in glory by means of Wadjet,
Who is beautiful by means of his great eye,
Which is under his eyebrow.
Verily, she guides the nine bows
Even when she issues commands to the nine troops;
And she causes the powers of [Apophis],
Who is in the darkness outside, to flee
Even when she puts slaughter
And blood of her into her enemies
In her name of "blood-red."

Let the Coiled One awaken even in peace,
With the awakening of your spirit (Ba)
Being in a state of peace!
You [the diadem] have been established
On the head of Sobek, etc,
Even so that you might appear in his forehead
In your name of "Great of Magic."
Let the gods have fear of you,
And let the living and the dead fall upon their faces for you!

1. Awake in peace! Great Queen, awake in peace;
thine awakening is peacefull.

2. Awake in peace! Snake that is on the brow of a king,
awake in peace; thine awakening is peaceful

3. Awake in peace! Upper Egyptian snake,
awake in peace, thine awakening is peaceful.

4. Awake in peace! Renenutet, awake in peace;
thine awakening is peaceful.

5. Awake in peace! Uto (the Dawn) splendidly fingered,
awake in peace; thine awakening is peaceful.

6. Awake in peace! Thou with head erect, with wide neck,
Awake in peace; thine awakening is peaceful.

7. Awake in peace! Thou with head erect, with graceful neck,
Awake in peace; thine awakening is peaceful.

8. Awake in peace! Selket,
Awake in peace; thine awakening is peaceful.

9. Awake in peace! Scribe, who binds the papyrus bundle,
Awake in peace; thine awakening is peaceful.

10. Awake in peace! Who points to the place in the fields,
Awake in peace; thine awakening is peaceful.

11. Awake in peace! Royal Serpent,
Awake in peace; thine awakening is peaceful.

Notes & Sources:

Broekhuis, Jan (1971) *De Godin Renenwetet*, Bib Classical Vangacumiana vol 19. English summary available; *The Edwin-Smith Surgical Papyrus*, col 18/15-16; *The Ebers Surgical Papyrus; Harris Magical Papyrus* (Col 10/1 – 11/1); Sauneron, Serge (1989) *Un Traité Egyptien d'Ophiologie* has six magical incantations to repel snakes. Red snakes here seen as manifestation of Set. The text includes a compendium of remedies, whose subsequent history is interesting in terms of medical alchemy – thus (p82) lists "sexualized" minerals – e.g.: "le mâle de galena". Sauneron, Serge (1962) *Les fêtes religieuses d'Esna au derniers siecles du paganisme*, Vol 5 (331 T 2 S); Khnum, Neith & Heka, Ptolemaic temple but extensive liturgy: Speech of Isis (p20&), Speech/Hymn of Thoth (p219); Birth of Apophis (p265); Uphill, Eric (1965) "The Egyptian Sed Festival Rites" *JNES* 24 p365-. Perhaps the nominal number of 30 dynasties is similarly modelled on the lunar month? The geomantic structure is recorded in scenes for Festival Hall of King Osorkon at Bubastis: The king takes his stand on the "staircase of the south" – South: Tjanen & Set; East: Isis & Nephthis; North: Atum & Horus; West: Kephra & Geb. Neville, E (1892) *Festival Hall of Osorkon II*; *Medinet Madi – (Narmouthis) shrine to Sobek, Horus & Renenutet*. Johnson, Sally B. *The Cobra Goddess of Ancient Egypt*. Raven, M J (1982) 'Corn Mummies' *OMRO* 63, 7.38

Unusual image of Khonsu, from R V Lanzone, *Dizionario di mitologia egizia*, 3 vols. Lanzone says the original is among the Turin Egyptian Museum's fifteen thousand small objects - so still looking.

Month 9 (March – April)
Khonsu "The wanderer"

The sun god Ra is all, more than just the visible sun, his Mysteries include the sun at midnight, the moon, his left-eye. Khonsu is the ancient moon god who gives his name to this month. To those that love him he is also the centre of the universe, thus Queen Cleopatra commissioned the following cosmological inscription for the temple of Khonsu at Karnac:

Khonsu
King of Upper and Lower Egypt
Moon, Pillar of Heaven
To your right I see the gods marching in
Montu, entering your left eye on the 1st lunar day
Atum, entering your left eye on the 2nd lunar day
Shu, entering your left eye on the 3rd lunar day
Tefnut, entering your left eye on the 4th lunar day
Geb, entering your left eye on the 5th lunar day
Nuit, entering your left eye on the 6th lunar day
Thoth entering your left eye on the 7th lunar day
Nephthys entering your left eye on the 8th lunar day

To your right I see the gods marching in
Osiris, entering your left eye on the 9th lunar day
Isis, entering your left eye on the 10th lunar day
Horus, entering your left eye on the 11th lunar day
Hathor, entering your left eye on the 12th lunar day
Sobek, entering your left eye on the 13th lunar day

Tjenenet, entering your left eye on the 14th lunar day
Iunyt, entering your left eye on the 15th lunar day

Cleopatra, the Queen, the lady of the two lands
stands to your left,
May your kindly face be gracious to me and to my beloved son
The Kings of Upper and Lower Egypt
stand to your left,
The sky is clear and the horizon
bears the form of the moon.
So that the left eye shines for everybody.
The sky is clear,
when the sound eye, born of Nuit, is elevated.

The following ancient invocation of Khonsu is another that makes use of a suitably filled cup; hold this in your hands to draw down the lunar blessings.

I am the one who appears shining and endures
My body grows old when I delay
For I am the serpent that came forth from the Nun,
I am the proud Ethiopian,
I am rearing serpent of real gold,
There is honey on my lips;
That which I shall say cometh to pass.
I am Anubis, the baby creature;
I am Isis and I will bind him,
I am Osiris the drowned who is bound.
Save me from every danger
Protect me, heal me, give me love, praise and reverence

Into my cup here to-day.
Come to me, Isis, mistress of magic,
the great sorceress of all the gods.
Horus is before me, Nephthys as my diadem, . . .
Send the mighty lion sons of Mihos
Send the souls of god,
The souls of man,
The souls of the Underworld,
The souls of the horizon,
The spirits, the dead,
Come into my cup and tell me the truth to-day
Concerning that after which I am inquiring:
I summon all your souls and forms to the mouth
Of my vessel;
Let them talk with their mouths,
Let them speak with their lips,
Let them say about that which I ask
Come in to me,
South, North, West, East,
Every breeze of Amenti, for I am the fury of all these gods,
Whose names I have uttered here to-day,
Rouse them for me,
The drowned, the dead; let your soul and your form live for me
Even the fury of Apophis and her daughters I summon
from their places of punishment,
Let him make me answer to every word [about]
which I am asking here to-day in truth without
falsehood therein. Hasten,
quickly

Notes & Sources

For the unusual "Khonsu Theology" of Cleopatra III (161–101BCE) see *Epigraphic Survey, The Temple of Khonsu* Vol 2, Chicago University Press. It is inscribed over the doorway to the inner sanctuary of Khonsu's temple at Karnac, first hypostyle hall, north wall, lintel.

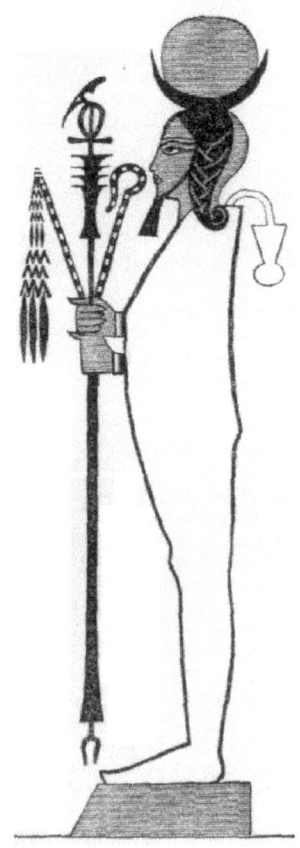

Khonsu, child avatar as part of the Theban triad with Amun & Mut. Illustration from J G Wilkinson, *Manners & Customs of the Ancient Egyptians*, 3 vols (Murray 1837)

Khenty Khet - an ancient lunar form of Horus. Illustration comes from R.V. Lanzone, (1881-6) *Dizionario di mitologia egizia*.

10th Month (April – May) Khentykhet – (Horus)

Khentykhet (Gr: Kentechtai) is an ancient lunar form of Horus, whose cult centre was Athribis in the Delta. There is a record of the visit of the Nubian Pharaoh Piankhi of 8th BCE to Athribis at the invitation of the local ruler that he "may see Khentykhet and worship his consort Khuyet offering an oblation of bulls, calves and fowl to Horus in his house." (BAR IV 867)

Khentykhet means "possessor of the divine body". He is especially associated with the crown and attributes of royalty including divine justice (Maat). In modern esotericism, the crown, in the wider sense of the head, signifies a person's self-esteem. Not surprising that this ancient ritual comes from a New Kingdom collection of spells for protection and general well being. This is the era of the Ramesside Kings, most famous of whom are Ramses II and his father Sety I.

Horus the moon (Khentykhet), is very much the chthonic counterpart of Horus the Sun (Khenty-Irty). So this ancient rite has strong lunar component and may be done whilst gazing on the full moon, drawing it down into one's crown or forehead. The spell mentions a special book from which one may recite the spell to the moon.

Whensoever I read this book,
It is for me a favoured day.
I will not hunger or experience thirst;
Neither will I know sorrow.

My heart is not afflicted;
For I am not imprisoned
Neither is judgement delivered against me;
If ever I go to gaol,
I come out vindicated;
Adorations are offered to me as if I am a god;
From whom affection is never parted.

I will not be overcome by my sorrows;
And the plague of the year will not harm me
Nor oppression crush me down.

Hail to you
Horus who resides at Athribis
Who, in the midst of all the gods;
judges the two lands in your boat
The jackal of the south,
"Opener of the Ways" who strikes the rebel;
Journeying in your shrine
As it roams in ancient places.

Mnervis Bull who rejuvenates,
Great god, master of Nubia
For whom Punt was created

To whom the two countries were given
So that he can rejoice in your own name.

Keep me away from evil
Protect me from all things bad and pernicious,
Done against me, or to my detriment;
Deliver me from the destruction of Sekhmet;
Protecting me from her red darts.

I am the one who avenges my father;
My form is your form
My places are your places
My heritage also yours.

I am one with Thoth,
Who made the alphabet,
Wearing the Crown of Ra,
As master of Heiracleopolis.
I am Ra
"He who makes himself secret to those who are in the Nun",
Firing arrows at enemies,
To destroy the reactionaries.

Jubilations for Horus-Khenty in Athribis,
Travel in peace.
I come near you; hear my call;
Grant me a long and properous life,
In the places I call home,
As do you in your beloved town.

Notes & Sources

My primary source is Vernus, Pascal (1978), *Athribis : textes et documents relatifs à la géographie, aux cultes, et à l'histoire d'une ville du delta Égyptien à l'époque pharaonique* from which I've translated the invocation which itself comes from Borghouts, J. F. 1978. *Ancient Egyptian Magical Texts*. Leiden: E. J. Brill. I also took information from Cauville, Sylvie (1983) *La théologie d'Osiris à Edfou* (Cairo). The latter is a commentary on the monumental Chassinat, Émile (1892-1985) *Le temple d'Edfou* that is the standard source on the site. Breasted, James Henry (1906-7) *Ancient records of Egypt: historical documents from the earliest times to the Persian conquest / collected, edited and translated with commentary* IV p.867. Wepwawet "Opener of the Ways" = Greek Ophois/Ophais.

Hippo Goddess from astrological ceiling of Senmut, Neugebauer O & Parker, R (1962) *Ancient Egyptian Astronomical Texts*, 4 vols, Brown University.

11th Month (May-June)
Ipet Hippo goddess

The feast for the hippopotamus goddess Ipet or Jepet ('her majesty') extended over two days but from New Kingdom times was celebrated in the first day of the month. There is a small temple of Ipet in the south-western corner of the temple complex at Karnak. She was also worshiped at Oxyrinchus and the Dakhleh Oasis along with her consort Set. She was an ancient Mother goddess, perhaps originally from Heliopolis, a tradition continued as birth goddess Thoeris. Her protective powers may also be invoked during sleep and in the dream landscape. Another of her names, especially in astrological texts is Reret "The Sow" and it is as well to recall that the Ancient Egyptians considered the Hippo to be a species of pig.

The following short hymn and spell was found on a small ostracon included in the published edition of Papyrus Turin:

Awake and embrace the void
Your heart strong enough for its joys
and its worries
Leave, and when you awake to life
You will feel young again on the new day
Rest, lie down assured of long good health.

"Good night,
the gods protect you,
their protection is before you each day

No bad thing approaches
The demon (Apep) is repelled from your bed chamber
Jepet the Great protects you in your long and powerful life."

The day and night illumined,
You shine forth
For she guides your steps on the right path,
And you know what is needed,
The god Ptah provisions you,
filling your storeroom,
With food and drink aplenty,
and in good measure.
Your diary and records all in order
and well composed.
The mistakes of the past forgotten,
The staff in your hand well made and sustaining.
Break bread with the wise,
Your cares all behind you.
Only reason lies before you,
The best is yet to come.

Praise be to TAWERET,
Bringing "perfection" in her beautiful name.
I praise her to the limits of the sky,
I desire her Ka, calming day by day.

Be merciful to me,
May I behold your mercy,
You, of perfect mercy!

Extend your hand to me,
Giving me life,
And granting me offspring!

Do not reproach me for my errors
You, in perfect mercy!
Even if my helpers slip up,
My peers still reward me.

I desire your great strength,
None knows you as I do;
I will say to the children and children's children:
Thee as guardian before her!

Joy my heart should seize,
Because on this day TAWERET is merciful,
My house prospers with her blessings.
May she give them day after day,
And I never say "Oh I have regrets!"

May she continue to give me health,
And my womb bear children safely,
[Or the future be secure].
My heart is glad every day, for sure
The good ones expel the evil,
And I am blessed.

Behold her people will live forever,
My enemies are fearful before you TAWARET!

Since your rage oppresses them
more than a mountain of iron,
Her mercy gives us life!

Notes & Sources

Jepet Hmt – most ancient form. Pleyte, Willem, *Papyrus Turin*, Brill, Ostacon p.1148 3-6 ; Daves, Norman G (1953) *Templi of Hiblis in El Khargeh*, Vol III; Bonnet, Hans, *Reallexikon* (RAAG) p530-535; Assmann, Jan, *Agyptische Hymnen*; Hornug, Erik & Theodor Abt *Knowledge of the Afterlife*; Jong, J Wde *Het Hat de Ipet* (Dutch with English summary).

Above: Ra at sunrise as Kephra, sunset as Tum. Detail from door lintel in tomb of Rameses X. The lower image is a very early version of the same idea, the mountains of sunrise/sunset, east/west. Nagada I/ Amratean predynastic pottery circa 4000BCE

12th Month (June-July) RaHorakhty or Ra

The vast majority of Egyptian hymns are devoted either to Osiris or to the sun god Ra in his various avatars. What follows are two examples, the first an extract, just one section of the voluminous *Litany of the Sun*. This litany survives in many versions but the standard text is taken from an inscription in the tomb of Sety I ("Belzoni's Tomb") in the Valley of the Kings, and therefore dating to c1350BCE. This is followed by a long solar ritual from the Greek Magical Papyri / Theban Magical Library.

The first text gives us an idea of the esoteric doctrine of the Egyptian priests, which was clearly pantheistic, and certainly differed from the polytheistic worship of the common people.

The second part uses a version from the Theban Magical Library in restored to the "original" Egyptian idiom. This invocation is rather long but one soon gets used to it. Almost every line implies a philosophical attitude and in order for the spell to work you have to have satisfied yourself that you understand and agree with this implicite theology. So even if you never use this spell - reading it, especially as part of a Pagan meditational practice is an important spiritual exercise.

I've shortened this some as I suspect that over time parts that were once instructions have become incorporated into the words of power. The vibe is an address to the sun, both visible and symbolic, as the pivot of the whole celestial hierarchy.

THE LITANY OF RA (1st Canto)

Title. The beginning of the book of the worship of RA in the West, (The heavenly region) of the worship of the United One in the West. When any one reads this book, porcelain figures are placed upon the ground, at the hour of the setting of the Sun, that is of the triumph of RA over his enemies in the West. Whoso is intelligent upon the earth, he is intelligent also after his death.

1 Homage to thee, RA ! Supreme power, the master of the hidden spheres who causes the principles to arise, who dwells in darkness, who is born as the all surrounding universe.

2 Homage to thee, RA ! Supreme power, the beetle that folds his wings, that rests in the empyrean, that is born as his own son.

3 Homage to thee, RA ! Supreme power, TANEN (The Earth) who produces his members (Gods), who fashions what is in him, who is born within his sphere.

4 Homage to thee, RA ! Supreme power, he who discloses the earth and lights the Ament, he whose principle has (become) his manifestation, and who is born under the form of the god with the large disk.

5 Homage to thee, RA ! Supreme power, the soul that speaks, that rests upon her high place, that creates the hidden intellects which are developed in her.

6 Homage to thee, RA ! Supreme power, the only one, the courageous one, who fashions his body, he who calls his gods (to life), when he arrives in his hidden sphere.

7 Homage to thee, RA ! Supreme power, he who addresses his eye, and who speaks to himself, he who imparts the breath of life to the souls (that are) in their place ; they receive it and develop.

8 Homage to thee, RA ! Supreme power, the spirit that walks, that destroys its enemies, that sends pain to the rebels.

9 Homage to thee, RA ! Supreme power, he who shines when he is in his sphere, who sends his darkness into his sphere, and who hides what it contains.

10 Homage to thee, RA ! Supreme power, he who lights the bodies which are on the horizon, he who enters his sphere.

Consecrating a ring, statue, etc., with the power of the sun god Ra

1. An address to the triple sun

I invoke and beseech the consecration,

O gods of the heavens

O gods under the earth

O gods circling on the middle region from one womb

O masters of all the living and dead

O heedful in many necessities of gods and men

O concealers of things now seen

O directors of Isis, Nemesis and Adrasteia who spend every hour with you

O senders of fate who travels around the whole world

O commanders of the rulers

O exalters of the abased

O revealers of the hidden

O guides of the winds

O arousers of the waves

O bringers of fire at the appropriate time

O creators and benefactors of every race

O Lords and controllers of kings

Come, benevolent ones, for the purpose for which I call you, as benevolent assistants in this rite for my benefit.

2. Assumption of the god form

I am an outflow of blood from the tomb of Osiris

[between] the palm trees

I am the faith found in men and I am he who declares the holy names, who is unchanging, who came forth from the abyss.
I am the sacred Phoenix bird
I am Helios
I am the god whom no one sees or rashly names
I am Shu the sender of winds
I am Tefnut the fire
I am Geb the earth
I am Nuit the mother of the gods
I am Osiris called water
I am Isis called dew
I am Set who defeats Apophis
I am Nephthys called spring
I am Harpocrates who came forth from the eye of the sun
I am an image resembling the true image
Therefore I beseech you
come as my helpers,
for I am about to call on the hidden and ineffable name, the forefather of the gods, overseer and lord of all

3. Hymn to the Demiurge

Come to me, you from the four winds,
god, ruler of all
who have breathed spirits into men for life,
master of the good things in the world.
Hear me, lord whose hidden name is ineffable.
The daimons, hearing it, are terrified -
the name is

BARBAREICH ARSEMPHEM-PHROTHOU

and of it the sun, of it the earth.
hearing, rolls over.
Hades, hearing is shaken
rivers, sea, lakes, springs, hearing are frozen
rocks, hearing it are split
Heaven is your head; ether body
earth feet and water around you ocean
O Agathos Daimon
You are lord, the begetter and nourisher and increaser of all

4. Hexametrical hymn to the Demiurge
Who molded the forms of the beasts of the Zodiac
Who found their routes
Who was the begetter of fruits?
Who raises up the mountains?
Who made the winds to hold to their annual tasks
What Aion nourishing an Aion rules the Aions?
One deathless god
You are the begetter of all and assign souls to all
and control all,
King of the Aions and Lord before who
mountains and plains
springs and rivers
valleys of earth
spirits and all things
High shining heaven
and every sea trembles.
Lord, ruler of all, holy one
and master of all.

By your power the elements exist
and all things come into being,
the route of the sun and moon,
of night and dawn
all things in air and earth and water and fire.
Yours is the eternal processional way of [heaven]
in which the seven lettered name is established for the harmony
of the seven sounds of the planets which utter their voices
according to the phases of the moon.
You give wealth, good old age, good children, strength, food.
You lord of life, ruler of the upper and lower realm,
whose justice is not thwarted,
whose glorious name the angels hymn,
who have truth that never lies,
hear me and complete for me this operation so that I may wear
this power in every place,
in every time, without being smitten or afflicted,
so as to be preserved intact from every danger
while I wear this power.
Yea lord, for to you,
the god in heaven,
all things are subject, and none of the daimons or spirits will
oppose me because I have called on your great name for the
consecrations.

5. Invocation of the deity

The gates of heaven are opened
The gates of earth are opened
The route of the sea is opened

The route of the rivers is opened
My spirit is heard by gods and daimons
My spirit is heard by the spirit of heaven
My spirit is heard by the terrestrial spirit
My spirit is heard by the marine spirit
My spirit is heard by the riverine spirit

Therefore give spirit to the ring
I have prepared
O gods whom I have named and called on
Give breath to the ring
Let its mouth be opened
so that it may breath and live
According to the Egyptian way: Ei IEOU - Oh Hail
According to the Jews: Ei IEOU - Oh Hail
According to the Greeks: Ei IEOU - Oh Hail
According to the High Priests of Egypt: Ei IEOU - Oh Hail
According to the Hindus - Ei IEOU - Oh Hail

Consecrate and empower this object for me,
for the entire and glorious time of my life.

Invoking the power of the sun

To use the ring or magical object there is a short invocation that one can recite whenever one has need of special power from the ring:

The gates of heaven are open
The gates of earth are open
The route of the sea

The route of rivers are opened
My spirit is was by all gods and daimons
My spirit is was by the spirit of heaven
My sprit is was by the terrestrial spirit
My spirit is was by the marine spirit
My spirit is was by the riverine spirit
Therefore give spirit to the mystery
I have prepared
O Gods whom I have named and have called on
Give breath to the mystery I have prepared.

Finish with a litany of 15 gods names. The text here is garbled, so I suggest some alternatives taken from the lunar days at the temple of Horus at Edfu:

EI IEOU Na (Oh Hail Red Serpent)
(pronounced Ai Ee-Ah-Ou with emphasis on the first syllable)
EI IEOU Shem (Oh Hail the stranger)
EI IEOU Irymeryef (Oh Hail the merry maker)
EI IEOU Wenet (Oh Hail The Hare Goddess)
EI IEOU Khnoum (Oh Hail)
EI IEOU Horus (Oh Hail his father's offspring)
EI IEOU Nehes (Oh Hail Goddess)
EI IEOU Thoth (Oh Hail)
EI IEOU Horus (Oh Hail avenger of his father)
EI IEOU Osiris (Oh Hail)
EI IEOU (Oh Hail) Amseti
EI IEOU (Oh Hail) Hapi
EI IEOU (Oh Hail) Tiamutef

EI IEOU (Oh Hail) Kebsenef
EI IEOU (Oh Hail) Iretef

Notes and Sources

The translation has been made from Edouard Naville, *La Litanie du Soleil* (Leipzig, 1875, avec un vol. de XLIX planches), where this text has been first translated into French with a commentary. Ring Spell from PGM XII 201-216 & 270-350. For Greek Helios as Egyptian Ra see Jacco Dielemann, *Priests, Tongues & Rites*, 2005 p159

Thoth (July/August)
Extra lunar month as needed, ie approximately every third year

By a quirk of history more is known of the popular cult of Thoth than its "official" temple version. For example Turin's Egyptian Museum (the largest outside Egypt) houses a small votive stele found at workman's village of the Theban necropolis (Deir el-Medina). This object tells us that one swore an oath by the moon and if one broke that oath, it was to the moon one appealed. It's a very human document and gives a glimpse at the world behind the perfect image presented in most "official" Egyptian inscriptions.

Spell to be said before portable shrine set before an image of the lunar barque bearing the moon's disk between two horns with caption "Lunar-Thoth: The great god, the merciful":

"I NN (*your name*) servant of the moon say:
'I am that man who uttered an oath
falsely by the Moon concerning [any matter].
And he caused me to see the greatness of
his power before the whole land.
I will declare thy might
To the fish of the deep
To the fowl of the skies
So they shall say to their children's children,
Be aware of the moon!
O merciful one, thou art able to turn this away".

Thoth - from Nubian tomb in I Rosellini, *Monumenti dell' Egitto e della Nubia* (Pisa 1832-44)

1. Standard Adoration to Thoth

O Gods who are in the sky
O Gods who are on the earth,
Gods of the south, north, west & east
Come and witness:
Thoth appear glorious with his crown (*oureret*)
in Hermopolis
With the Two Lords, Horus & Set
Guiding the common people (*rekhyt*)
Exultant in the great house of Geb, the earth god
On account of his efforts.
Adore him, exalt him, praise him!
Felicitous Lord,
The guide of the masses in their entirety
All you gods and goddesses, behold!
Praise Thoth this day
Who founded your sanctuaries,
And devised the temple liturgy
On the primal sunset island.

2. Greeting to you, Thoth!
It is me, alone (here), who adores you.
Give me a home and property
So that I am grounded with possessions.
Let me live,
In the country of the living,
Made by you on the primal sunset island.
Give me love, blessings, benevolence and protection;
This person here of feelings, mind and heart,

Whether commoner, patrician or astral being etc.
Overcome my enemies in this life or the next!
Said by offrant of Thoth,
One who is justified before his adversaries
In the tribunal of the Gods
Over which Thoth presides,
Commanding the nine (Gods) of the Company of Heaven.

2. Prayer to Thoth

O Thoth, take me to Hermopolis
The city where the living is easy,
And I am placed before the Lord my god
And I go forth justified.
Where you provide all the necessities of life,
In bread and beer.
Come, O divine speech!
Thoth, you are behind me in the morning!
Guarding my mouth (when) I speak.

O great sixty cubit doum-palm
Which bears a fine crop,
Of luscious fruits within every
moist kernal.

O you who provide water in desert,
Come and save me, who keeps silent!
O Thoth, gentle fountain in the desert!
Untouched by human artifice.
The one that is hidden from the profane,

But flows for the initiate,
who comes silently to the well spring.

3. Prayer to Thoth
Praise be thou, O Lord of the house,
Baboon radiant of mane,
of sweet appearance and gentle charm,
beloved of everybody.
You of the *shrt*-stone
Shine on Thoth and illuminate
the land in all its beauty.
Upon your head is the crown of red jasper
and your phallus of cornelian.
Love emanates from your brow,
And when you speak you bestow life.
My threshold is blessed when the dog (*iw*) enters.
It thrives and has flourished from the time
that my lord has trodden it.
Be happy you of my street,
Rejoice all my neighbours.
Behold my lord, it is he who has made me,
thus my heart longs for him.
Thoth, thou shall be my companion,
and I shall never fear the (evil) eye.

4. Prayer of a scribe of Thoth
Come to me Thoth, august ibis,
Desired God of Hermopolis,
Scribe of the acts of the Company of Heaven.

Great in your city!
Help me to direct myself,
Making me skilful in our profession.
The best of all occupations.
It rises one up.
The respected scribe becomes great.
There are many you have thus helped;
Who are now among the best,
Your actions are strong and graceful.
You are the one who guides a person ,
who lacks a mother's hand.
Fate and Renenutet are beside you.
Come and guide me.
An attendant of your temple.
Allow me to impart your knowledge ,
Such that in any country where I am,
The multitude of people say;
Great is the knowledge of Thoth!
And they come, together with their children,
To be marked (branded) as scribes:
The good profession of the victorious Lord!
Happy the one who exercises it!

Notes & Sources:

Claas J Bleeker, *Hathor & Thoth, Two Key Figures in Ancient Egyptian Religion*, Leiden 1973; Patrick Boyland, *Thoth the Hermes of Egypt* London 1922; Battiscombe Gunn "The religion of the Poor in Ancient Egypt" *JEA* III p 81-94. Adolf Erman, *Handbook of*

Egyptian Religion; translated by A S Griffith; André Barucq & A F Daumas, *Hymnes et prières d'Egypt*, Paris 1980; Gardiner, A H, *Late Egyptian Miscellanies,* Bruxelles 1937. The terms feeling, mind and heart in the first prayer are translations of Hwt "to burn"; HAty = "thoughts, mind"; Ib = "heart".) The third hymn is translated by Ricardo A. Caminos in his thesis/translation of Allan Gardiner's, *Late-Egyptian miscellanies.* "The Evil Eye" is literally *'Irt* - the "left eye of heaven, the moon".

Figure 14: Astronomical ceiling from temple of Ramses II (Ramesseum) at Luxor, circa 1290-1223 bce.

This 9.10m x 3.90m ceiling comes from the east-west axis of the 2nd hypostyle hall, the so-called Astronomical Room. A H Gardiner suggests this might have been a library. The complicated panel is to be read from the eastern corner.

It is divided into three bands - the upper or southernmost is a list of planets and decans. This rising or culmination of the decans and planets was used to determine the hours of the night. The rising or culminating decan was also an indicator of the fate of those born during that hour - the precursor to later developments in astrology.

The central band shows the northern constellations and deities of the lunar days.

The lower or northernmost band is a lunar calendar. The king is shown officiating with the deities of each month.

Other features: A laudatory inscription borders the entire panel. Between this and the top band of planets and decans can be seen the names of each month in hieroglyphic script. The month names as transcribed in Chapter 2 - Table 5

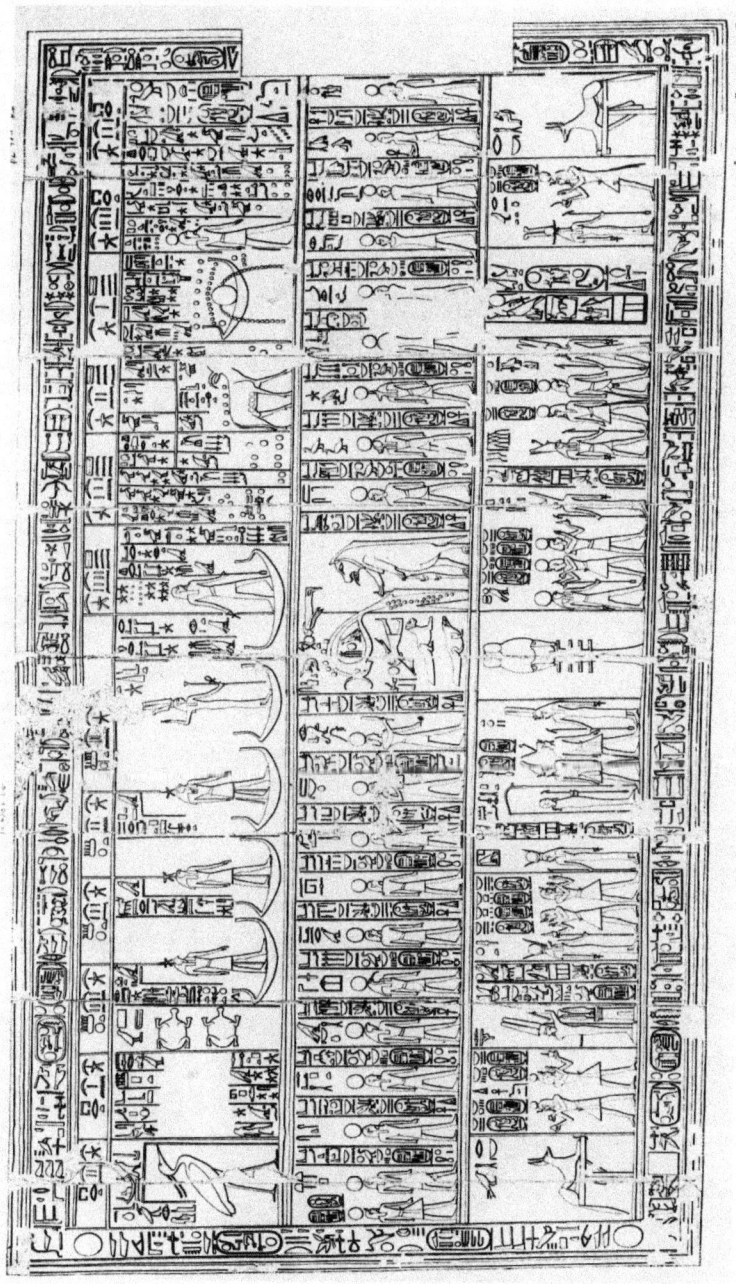

Notes

1. Parker (1950 : 34)

2. Set is included in the epagomenal days but these have an inauspicious character and it is unlikely if Set's day was ever marked in the official calendars of later pharaonic times.

3. Morgan (2005 : 180)

4. Borghouts, J (1987 : 39) 'Akhu and Hekau' in *La Magia in Egitto ai Temple dei Faraoni*, ed Roccati A & Siliotti

'The Egyptians hold solemn assemblies not once in the year, but often. The chiefest of these and the most zealously celebrated is at the town of Bubastis in honour of Artemis, and the next is that in honour of Isis at Busiris. This town is in the middle of the Egyptian Delta, and there is in it a very great temple of Isis, who is in the Greek language, Demeter. The third greatest festival is at Sais in honour of Athene; the fourth is the festival of the sun at Heliopolis; the fifth of Leto at Buto, and the sixth of Ares at Papremis.'

Herodotus Book II : 50
(translation Godley)

2 The Later Festival Year

In this chapter we will study the Ancient Egyptian religious year in more detail. My aim is to present the reconstructed festival calendar used *after* the lunar version was abolished, that is to say, for pretty much all of Egypt's recorded history. This task is tricky. It would be handy if I could simply refer the reader to a reliable summary of the basics. You would think after more than a century of academic and popular writing, there would be a standard work on the hidden and essential key to Egyptian magical thought. But I have found nothing in the realm of popular writings that I can 100% recommend. For example the recently published *Egyptian Book of Days* is misleading, as it takes as a source one of the many *Almanacs of Lucky and Unlucky Days*, which though interesting in their own right, are a poor guide to the ancient Egyptian religious year. These almanacs omit certain important feasts such as *Thoth* and *Wag*, perhaps because they were so well known! Technical, academic studies on the Egyptian religious year are complex, assuming a great deal of prior knowledge and are often expensive or difficult to acquire.

This is my justification for what some might see as stating the obvious. It will also be a contrast to the archaic lunar-stellar calendar introduced in chapter 1. The lunar-stellar calendar was connected with the mythology of the god Set. The new solar calendar was created to reflect the new reality of a unified Egypt and the rise of the cult of Osiris. Aspects of the older lunar calendar were always preserved by the Egyptians thus *some* of it continued to influence what came after, right up until the modern day.

Basic concepts such as the week, the months etc

Margaret Murray is one of the few to mention that the Egyptians divided the month into three weeks of ten days each duration. This division is related to *Star Clocks* and observation of 'decanal' stars. This division might be more theoretical than practical. I have so far failed to find any inscription that makes an everyday reference to the weeks. In our own modern culture it is only really in some specialist environments such as the university year, where one finds any reference to time in terms of weeks. So it might be something that was understood but never referred to, similar in a way to which, as we shall see, the ancient Egyptians referred to the month by a number, eg: I Akhet 20 and reserved the month's name (e.g. Thoth) for spoken discourse.

The workers of the Ramesside colony at Deir el Medina worked a ten day week. They worked ten hours days, with one break. Two of the ten days were rest days. For this the workers were paid partly in food and lodging, and partly in cloth.[1] Papyrus Reisner is a detailed New Kingdom 'payroll'. Accounts for individual workers are arranged over the thirty days of the month with no obvious indication of weeks or rest days. It might be that these hieroglyphic numbers indicate weeks:

week one	I	II	III
week two	∩I	∩II	∩III
week three	∩∩I	∩∩II	∩∩III

From these work rosters we discover one [ordinal] day name - the last or thirtieth day areky (ʿrky) perhaps because it is a day of reckoning.[2]

Nilsson[3] says that the tripartite division of the month is also the natural one attested from anthropological studies cited in his crucial book: *Primitive Time Reckoning*. The days of the full moon naturally fall thus:

days   1 - 10   The rise
days   11 - 20   'white nights'
days   21 - 30   The fall

The month names

The names and order of the Egyptian months are as follows:

1   Thoth
2   Phaophi
3   Athyr
4   Choiak
5   Tybi
6   Mechir
7   Pharmenoth
8   Pharmuthi
9   Pachons
10 Payni
11 Epiphi
12 Mesore

There is a modern convention that lists these alongside their equivalents from the later Julian calendar. The following table shows this, but please bear in mind these are conventions and are only the equivalents utilized in the first century of the common era. The Julian month names are by no means translations of the Egyptian originals - that will come later.

Nilsson[4] reminds us that ancient month names tend to follow the phases and occupations of the natural year. The ancient Egyptian month names bear the names of gods - but each of these probably had some connection with the agricultural year, the planting and harvesting etc. More of this below.

The Three Seasons

The ancient Egyptians later came to group their months into three distinct seasons:

Egyptian seasons	Julian month
Akhet (inundation)	Jul
	Aug
	Sep
	Oct
Peret (winter)	Nov
	Dec
	Jan
	Feb
Shemu (summer)	Mar
	Apr
	May
	Jun

Nilsson[5] thought that Egyptian schema of three seasons may even have influenced the Indian model. India famously has six seasons but these are grouped in a way that reveals an underlying tripartite model. Whilst on the topic of Egypt's Indian legacy - it might be worth remembering that the Ayurvedic medical system utilises an matrix of humours said to predominate in certain seasons. This East-West parallel might help in the process of reconstructing the ancient Egyptian medical model, which has already revealed many striking similarities with Ayurvedic medicine. The Egyptians and the Indo-Iranians who brought Ayurveda to India may well have shared some common cosmological ideas concerning the elements and some notions of disease causation.[6]

The entire array of seasons, Egyptian months and putative Julian equivalents are set out in Table 2:

The Egyptian Festival Year

I assume that readers of this book are in some way wanting to re-enact the religious life of the ancient Egyptians. Therefore you should know that festivals in ancient Egypt fell into two main categories.

1. Feasts of the seasons (*hebew tep terew*)

2. Feasts of heaven (*hebew new pet*)

Feasts of heaven are those celebrations connected with the phases of the moon. Incidentally several books say that the moon played little or no part in Egyptian religion. I don't think that it is true and suspect that what follows will remove this misunderstanding. Apart from the moon, it might also be convenient to place other astronomically determined feasts under this heading, most famously the celebration of the heliacal rising of Sirius. But

Table 2: The Ancient Egyptian Civil Year					
A	B	C	D	E	F
	Egyptian seasons	Months of Egyptian civil year	Hieroglyphic transcription	Associated dieties	Julian month
0					
I		Thoth	*dhwty*	Thoth	Jul
II	Akhet	Phaophi	*p n jpt*	Opet	Aug
III	(inundation)	Athyr	*Hwt-hr*	Hathor	Sep
IV		Choiak	*k3 hr k3*	Osiris	Oct
I		Tybi	*t3 ᶜbt*		Nov
II	Peret	Mechir	*mhyr*		Dec
III	(winter)	Pharmenoth	*p n jmn htp*	Amunhotep	Jan
IV		Pharmuthi	*p n rnwtt*	Renenutet	Feb
I		Pachons	*p n hnsw*	Khonsu	Mar
II	Shemw	Payni	*p n jnt*		Apr
III	(summer)	Epiphi	*ipip*	Ipet	May
IV		Mesore	*mswt rᶜ*	Ra or Ra Horakhty	Jun

Column A-B: in written records the Egyptians only used the 'seasonal names' eg 'I peret 15' although they may have used names such as Tybi or Mechir in normal speech much as we would vocalise 1/1/06 as 1st Jan 2006. (Depuydt 1977 : 59)

Column C: these names appear in Greek, Roman and Coptic sources although hardly ever in native sources from which they ultimately derive.

Column D: this hieroglyphic version is taken from Mss Cairo 86637 and was based on one of Egypt's lunar calendars. but just like our own months they have lost all but their linguistic connection to the

Column E: Ipet and Opet are homonyms distinguished here by a variation in spelling - in Egyptian there is no such difference. Ipet is an ancient hippo goddess. Opet is a goddess associated with the

Table 2: The Ancient Egyptian Civil Year

to confound the orderly minded this particular feast was grouped by the Egyptians along with feasts of the seasons.

There are three other important type of feast that we should at least note here even if we are not going to discuss them in any detail. These are

3. Regional feasts
4. Political feasts
5. Individual feasts

1. Feasts of the seasons

Throughout their entire *written* history the ancient Egyptians used a seasonal calendar consisting of twelve months, each of 30 days duration. As 12 x 30 = 360 days this is approximately five days shorter than it needs to be to keep pace with the solar year. Evidence of the very earliest Pyramid Texts (circa 2350BCE) show that from the time of Egypt's unification five extra or *epagomenal* days were added to the year. These epagomenal days are really a calendrical convention. Just to make things more complicated the birthdays of several major Egyptian gods were allocated to each of these days. These five days, coming as they do between the old and new year were considered a dangerous time, necessitating apotropaic rites of the kind recorded in various places, including the *Cairo Calendar* or *Alamanac of Lucky and Unlucky Days* (see *Supernatural Assault in Ancient Egypt*).

The addition of these five extra days on the solar year is not quite enough to keep things in order. This is because the annual *apparent* orbit of the sun around the earth actually takes 365 + almost one quarter day (actually 365.2422 days). So the first thing the Egyptians noticed soon after the inauguration of their new calendar, was that it lost a day every four years! They couldn't have failed to notice this but did nothing about it. There was no 'leap' year until the coming of the Romans and the death of the last Pharaoh Cleopatra.

The year was simply allowed to wander. Hence it is sometimes known as the wandering year or if your prefer to use Jan Assmann's term a 'virtual year'. It rolls on, year after year, loosing ever more and more days, so that after 120 years it has wandered a full month behind. Some feasts such as the Heliacal Rising of Sirius and High Nile remained as moveable feasts because of their inextricable link with natural phenomenon. Most others, for instance New Year's day, shed their astrological moorings and could be celebrated often months before their original raison d'etre! It takes approximately 1460 years for such a calendar to come full circle. In the meantime, it is as if Yule or Christmas were celebrated in the summer, or harvest festival in the spring.

This didn't seem to bother the ancient Egyptians - but it probably does bother you. It would be particularly bothersome to the neo-pagan, whose existence is predicated on a return to nature and natural phenomena. Can it be that the ancient Egyptians were so divorced from the facts of nature? Well yes it is true - the Egyptians throughout most of their history had very little concern about these issues. In this 'denial' of nature, they were similar in attitude to the Romans. If you want to find the more pagan, nature orientated Egyptians, you will have to look elsewhere - including amongst the much maligned Sethians.

Although the beginning of the year, known as I Akhet 1 (Thoth), was supposedly heralded by the Heliacal Rising of Sirius or Sothis, the facts were somewhat different. There was a rupture between observable facts and the calendar. The list of holy 'red letter' days may have lost their connection to reality - but they were still celebrated with gusto.

As I mentioned, the Romans made a calendar reform and 'leap' year under Julius Ceasar, the so-called Julian calendar. This required one further reform in 1582 by Pope Gregory. Universal adoption of his schema took some time, for example not before 1752 in Britain and its 'possessions'.

But essentially when dealing with Egyptian dates, it is the Julian calendar that is read back in time and provides the nominal annual equivalents for the Egyptian civil calendar. The whole schema is set out in **Table 3**:

Despite its conventional nature, the Egyptian civil calendar does have several interesting features. For instance, the months are each named after the deity whose feast once fell in that, or is otherwise related to that month. The names of months are thus said to be 'Theophoric' or 'god bearing'. The way they are named betrays their origins in the Old Kingdom, arguably even before the unification of Egypt. That is to say, very ancient origins indeed. These are the clues we will used earlier to reconstruct at least one, perhaps two original and archaic lunar calendars.[7]

This 'god bearing quality' is easiest to recognise in month names three, eight and nine which are consistently linked with Hathor, Renenutet the harvest goddess and Khonsu the moon god respectively. Whilst there are several variations in the correspondence between gods and the other Egyptian months, these three never seem to change. We are therefore confronted here by a very strong tradition. Unless you are familiar with the hieroglyphic transcription this may not exactly jump off the page - but the Egyptian name *hewet-her* become Hathor in Greek; *renewtet* becomes Greek Renenutet and *ḥnsw* is Khonsu. The Greek month names preserve the original Egyptian Athyr = Hathor; Pharmenoth, slightly more tricky but must be derived from Egyptian *pe en renewtet* - meaning 'the one of Renenutet' and Greek month name Pachons comes from Egyptian *pe en ḥnsw* meaning 'the one of Khonsu'.

Incidentally, it is a feature of Egyptology that some of the very latest texts and monuments often incorporate very ancient traditions. For example, those buildings commissioned by Egypt's Greek rulers are very archaic in style. It is quite likely that the famous Greek Library of Alexandria (rumoured to have been partly destroyed by Julius Ceasar in 48BCE) contained some of the very oldest of papyrus manuscripts. The Ptolemaic dynasty was founded in 305BCE. One by-product of the Ptolemies' love of ancient wisdom, was a tendency to use old and now lost manuscript originals as sources of the astronomical decoration of temples, as can be seen at Dendera and Edfu. Extremely old pieces of knowledge from Egypt's beginnings often sit alongside relatively modern innovations, such as the Zodiac. The Zodiac as we still know it was probably a Greek innovation, although as I shall show,

Table 3: The Festival Year

	Egyptian	Months of civil year	Day	Feast	Hiero-glyphs	Deities	
I	Akhet - Inundation	Thoth	1	for new year	wp rnpt		Jul
			18	of Wagy*	dhwty		
			19	of Thoth		Thoth	
			20	of drunkenness			
			22-	Great procession of Osiris			
II		Phaophi	15	of Opet	p n jpt	Opet	Aug
			25	of Ptah	pth	Ptah	
			17, 25	of clothing	mnht		
III		Athyr	30	of Hathor	Hwt-hr	Hathor	Sep
IV		Choiak	25-	of Sokar / Osiris	k3 hr k3	Osiris	Oct
			?	of Sekhmet			
I	Peret - Planting	Tybi	1	Nehebkau	t3 ʿbt		
			18-28	of Mut's departure			Nov
				of sacrifice			
II		Mechir	1	of clothing	mhyr		Dec
			?	of Anubis			
III		Pharmenoth	1	Great fire festival	p n jmn htp	Imenhotep	Jan
			1	of Ptah			
			?	of Amen-hotep			
IV		Pharmuthi	1	Lesser fire festival	p n rnwtt	Renenutet	Feb
			1	of Bastet			
I	Shemu - Harvest	Pachons	1?	of Khonsu	p n hnsw	Khonsu	Mar
			1	of Renenutet			
			1	of Min			
II		Payni		of Khenti-khety	Hnt-hty		Apr
III		Epiphi		Valley feast			May
IV		Mesore	1-2	of hippopot-amus goddess Ipet	ipip	Ipet	Jun
			30	of opening of the year	mswt rʿ	Ra or Ra Horakhty	
Five epagomenal days							
day 1	Birth of Osiris						Jul
day 2	Birth of Horus						
day 3	Birth of Seth						
day 4	Birth of Isis						
day 5	Birth of Nephthys						

Table 3: The Festival Year

this innovation was in part driven by knowledge of the Egyptian proto-zodiac. We can but wonder at what was lost in that famous fire - assuming it happened!

Returning then to the topic of the standard Egyptian festival calendar. **Table 2** presents the twelve months of the year with some of their corresponding deities. If your favourite is in the list, then you have a clue as to when to celebrate their feast day. But as there are more than twelve gods in ancient Egypt, things may get a little bit more complex. But for the sake of discussion, in **Table 3** is a reconstructed festival calendar as it might have been before it was banned by the Romans in 4th century of our era. The Romans have the strange role in this narrative of providing some firm if arbitrary dates for these feasts, whilst driving the final nail into the Egyptian religious coffin.

In what follows, I am going to have to ask you to ignore what I have just said concerning the names of the months and their link with particularly gods. The simple fact is that because of the transfer of these dates to the new festival calendar, they are often celebrated 'out of sequence' - overriding any older association between month and god. The festivities were determined more by what we might call bureaucratic considerations, much as in the way United Kingdom 'bank holidays' are set. For example, our May Day bank holiday ought to be on the first of May. For many years there was no May Day bank holiday. Currently, it is always a monday, thus in 2004, it was celebrated on the third rather than first of May. Indeed, our modern calendar owes a great deal to the innovations of the ancient Egyptians.[8]

The Reconstructed Festival Calendar

I Akhet (Thoth) - July

Day 1: New Year. Is it celebration of New Year, or end of the Old Year, or the space in between? It was certainly both celebration and propitiation for a dangerous time between the years. I have appended the details at this epagomenal period at the end of the chapter.

Day 18: Wagy - the importance of this feast is attested from many inscriptions, but sadly other than its existence very little is known of its ritual form. It was originally a moveable lunar feast always occuring on the 18th lunar day. This was later transferred to the fixed festival calendar as the 18th day of the month of Thoth. It is attested from earliest times until its reform in the Ptolemaic period (305-30BCE). One meaning of Wag is 'to provision' and the annual resupply of the tombs of one's ancestors was undoubtedly a large part of this solemn feast. It is a time of offering, especially of new linen for the benefit of the ancestors. An additional meaning of Wag might be 'to whistle', and it is possible that the feast involved some form of chanting or 'keening' to the departed souls. This antique feast is inevitably influenced by the cult of Osiris, whose shrine at Abydos, and no doubt many a lesser shrine needed resupply. The linen of previous years was torn into strips and taken by pilgrims as divine relics. These green or purple bandages were much prized and are often referred to in inscriptions.

Wag was chiefly an evening feast, celebrated on the evening immediately before the 18th. Wag could also mean the keel of a boat. The boat in question is that which bears the body of Osiris on his final journey. I would remind you that the ancient Egyptians also slept on a 'keel' of folden linen, so there are multiple layers of meaning here. The morning after Wag was considered the Heb Sed of Osiris.[9]

Day 19: Thoth was exalted on the 19th day of his own month, the first of the year. The reason for this is not obvious. Spalinger[10] thinks this is because nineteen is the difference between 365 (the solar year) and 384 (the lunar year) ie -11 (or +19). For me there may be some additional rationale. Nineteen years is also a complete lunar cycle. This is supposedly the later discovery of Babylonian astronomy. The nineteen years consist of twelve years with twelve new moons and seven years with thirteen new moons. Thoth is also a moon god and thus could be considered the deity of the entire year.

Day 20: The feast of drunkenness. The association of this feast with the goddess Hathor seems to be a feature of a comparatively late stage of Egyptian history. There is no citation earlier than the Dendera feast lists, which despite all appearances are Ptolemaic. The Ptolemaic festival commemorates the return of Hathor from the Nubian desert.[11]

Drunkenness was considered a manifestation of the Sethian personality type:

> 'If he (the Sethian) drinks a beer, he drinks it to engender strife and turmoil. The redness of the white of his eye is this god. He is one who drinks what he detests.'[12]

Almanacs of Lucky & Unlucky Days also identify nativities which result in death by drunkenness - but this is not viewed as an inauspicious end:

> Akhet II, day 6 : f(avourable). f(avourable). f(avourable). A happy day for Ra in heaven, and the gods are pacified in his presence. The Ennead is making glorification in front of the Lord of the Universe. Anyone born on this day will die in a state of drunkenness. [13]

Although drunkenness may be seen as bad, intoxication was viewed as good, aiding communion with the dead and the gods.

Despite its placement on day twenty immediately after the Wag feast, there is no connection between the two. What is so special about day twenty in the civil calendar? Spalinger[14] the leading academic authority on Egyptian calendrics should be credited with having solved this long standing riddle. For reasons set out in the footnote - day twenty corresponded with the new moon. The feast of drunkenness was therefore almost certainly a new moon celebration, perhaps occurring at the beginning of the second lunar month.

II Akhet (Inundation) - Phaophi - August
Day 15: Feast of Opet

Very few details survive of the 'beautiful Feast of Opet' (*heb nefer en jepet*). The feast began on the *evening* before the 15th day of second civil month of Akhet and continued for pretty much the rest of the month. The 15th day is the full moon, thus it is reasonable to suppose this was originally a full moon feast, that continued for the remainder of the lunar fortnight. There are no records of this feast before the 18th Dynasty, but by the reign of queen Hatshepsut it was an annual event. It survived until the fall of paganism in Egypt, and there are echoes of it in subsequent Coptic literature.

There was a procession during which Amun of Karnak journeyed southward to the temple of his consort Mut at Luxor. In later times both journeys were by river. The outward one against the stream, was assisted by crowds of pilgrims towing the god's ceremonial barque. These strenuous activities were lightened by drinking songs whose origin is very ancient, far antedating Opet. The melee was also an occasion for oracular appeals to the god. What happens when Amun reached Luxor, is the subject of a great deal of speculation, especially concerning the role of a special priestess called 'God's Wife.' Possibilities include some form of sacred marriage involving sexual rites in the so-called 'birth room', in which the new king was conceived by Amun.[15]

The above feast probably replaced an older Memphite commemoration of Ptah, which is recorded for Esna as occurring on the 25 of the month, although other dates are known.

The Old Kingdom sun temple of Niuserre (2453-2422 BCE) lists a celebration connected with clothing. This is also mentioned in two Middle Kingdom inscriptions dated one year apart on 27 and 17 Phaophi. This ten day difference from one year to the next, is further evidence of a lunar calculation.

III Akhet (Inundation) - Athyr - September

There is a very ancient and sustained connection between the third month of the year, and the Goddess Hathor. Although for reasons that have become the subject of considerable debate, the major festival of Hathor actually occurs on the first day of the next month. This slippage is probably due to the transfer of feasts from an old lunar calendar, to the civil version. Coming as it does towards the end of the season of inundation, the river is more navigable and Hathor's month involves a great deal of activity on the river. The major boat shrines and escort vessels celebrate the return of nature in all its greenery - the rite of the sistrum (*zešzeš*) is done over the water from one of these boats. In its earliest form, this instrument's handle is shaped like the stem and bud of the papyrus plant - hence the term 'shaking the papyrus' (*zešzeš waḏ*).

The most prominent festival was her sacred marriage as Mistress of Dendera to Horus of Edfu. Her cult statue was taken by boat to Edfu, arriving on the new moon and lingering 13 days until just before the full moon.[16]

IV Akhet (Inundation) - Choiak - October

Sokar is an ancient god connected with the Memphite necropolis, whose cult was eventually assimilated to that of Osiris. He appears as a human figure wrapped in mummy cloths but with a hawk's head. The origins and meaning of his name are obscure and may disguise a more archaic agricultural or fertility deity as well as patron of craftsmen. There is a long association between death and the fertility of the land, very reminiscent of the European myth of John Barleycorn.

The festival consists of several heterogenous celebrations with agricultural character such as hoeing the earth. By the 5th Dynasty, the Sokar festival is largely assimilated to the cult of Osiris. These mysteries all occur in the dark or waning half of the month on various days depending on which religious centre is studied. These festivities include the famous procession of Osiris at Abydos, circumambulation of temple walls, raising of Djed pillars etc.[17]

The dead Osiris is the vanished moon. His day of embalmment is the day when the moon is never visible. But on the following day, Choiak 25, he shines forth from his temple at sunset, just as the crescent moon normally appears on the second day of the lunar month at sunset. If this be the resurrection of Osiris, which it certainly seems to be since he wakes from his sleep and takes his place in the sky, then it is small wonder that Horus, son of Osiris, is born on the same lunar day on which his father is reborn.[18]

In this month, fell the feast of goddess Sekhmet for which details are scanty.

I Peret (Winter) – Tybi – November
Day 1
The previous month's Sokar feast perhaps sets the scene for the feast of Nehebkau on the first day of Tybi. Nehebkau is another 'opener of the year' which can also be an occasion for celebrations connected with the Egyptian monarchy.

This second new year feast falls under the auspices of the God (or demon) Nehebkau. Indeed, Spalinger thinks that Nehebkau was the name for this month in the original lunar calendar. This 'demon' decorates the throne of the goddesses Sekhmet and Bastet. The meaning of the name is 'bestower of dignities'. The serpentine god appears as early as the Pyramid Texts (PT 487). His consort is Serket the scorpion goddess - who is also sometimes paired with Seth. All this serves to underline the ambiguous nature of Nehebkau, as a divine entity with demonic attributes. He was perhaps in origin an associate of the storm deity Apophis - whom he closely resembles. Nehebkau was another serpent demon enemy of Ra, brought on side in some lost mythological incident. This explains Nehebkau's position in the throne of the mighty Sekhmet, who alongside Seth is powerful enough to vanquish Apophis. Serpents - demonic and otherwise - are encountered later in conjunction with the cult of the Decans, Egypt's proto-astrology.[19]

Some festival lists mention an otherwise unspecified 'Great Feast' falling in this month over several days. We could perhaps link this with the great feast of Horus of Edfu, that fell on the first day of Tyby, presumably also a new moon feast. This may have replaced the lesser of two ancient 'fire festivals'. Under this heading, could be included various activities on the river in festival boats in which the god's enemies were repelled by a symbolic 'thirty spears'. Other gods may also have received an outing on the river in their ceremonial barque. These include: Uto, Bastet, Hathor and Mut - all occuring in dark half of the month ie between 18-28th day.

II Peret (Winter) - Mechir - December (older name= Rekhwer)

Mechir meaning 'clothing'. I mentioned above a similar or perhaps related feast of clothing that crops up in the records of King Neuserre. This happened in the second month of the previous season - II Akhet (Phaophi). But in even older records, it was the occasion of a Great Fire Festival, probably falling on the new moon, details of which are unknown. This is the coldest time of the year, hence the necessity for the bonfire and indeed the explanation of the reference to clothing. Harvested fields were cleared by stubble burning.

In this month, perhaps on the new moon, could also be placed a festival of Anubis (although this might be a hangover from the various 'going forths' of the previous month). The clothing could also be associated with the process of wrapping the deceased in mummy cloth.

III Peret (Winter) - Pharmenoth - January (older name = rekh-nedes)

Day 1: Lesser Fire Festival

Again, still during the Egyptian winter, Old Kingdom calendars speak of a smaller fire festival, after the larger one of the previous month. How it was celebrated is largely unknown.

Also on this day in Memphis, falls the end of local celebrations for Ptah - god of craftsmen, who is credited with inventing the ceremony of opening the mouth. Names of his rites might give some clue as to their content - 'Ptah in his feast of raising the sky'

- perhaps an allusion to his creative activities. His cosmological role is overshadowed by the cult of Amun - whose feast takes the name 'Amun in his Festival of raising the sky' - (*Jemen em heh.ef en abej pet*).

The feast for the deified Amenhotep I (1545-1525BCE). He was the son of Ahmose, the second king of the 18th Dynasty who consolidated and strengthened his father's achievements, driving the Hiksos from Northern Egypt. Amenhotep reigned over a golden age of arts and culture and was venerated as a local god at Deir el Medina. By the 20th Dynasty his cult had become so popular it gave its name to the month.

IV Peret (Winter) - Pharmuthi - February

One would expect a feast, possibly involving fire, for the harvest goddess Renenutet, whose usual form is that of a woman wearing the serpentine uraeus headdress, or as a large snake wearing the solar disk and cow's horns. The association of snakes with harvested fields is perhaps a universal phenomenon, not to mention hazard that required some form of propitiation. However, her festival was more often celebrated in the following month.

Instead, we might find feasts for the Theban cat-goddess *Bastet* celebrated during this month, although at Bubastis, north of Cairo in lower Egypt, the feast was celebrated in the second month of the year viz: II Akhet. The following passage from Herodotus (Book II. 60-61) gives a flavour of these activities:

> 60. When the people are on their way to Bubastis they go by

river, men and women together, a great number of each in every boat. Some of the women make a noise with rattles, others play flutes all the way, while the rest of the women, and the men, sing and clap their hands. As they journey by river to Bubastis, whenever they come near any other town they bring their boat near the bank; then some of the women do as I have said, while some shout mockery of the women of the town; others dance, and others stand up and expose their persons. This they do whenever they come beside any riverside town. But when they have reached Bubastis, they make a festival with great sacrifices, and more wine is drunk at this feast than in the whole year beside. Men and women (but not children) are wont to assemble there to the number of seven hundred thousand, as the people of the place say.

I Shemu (Summer) - Pachons - March
Day 1 Feast of Renenutet

Since the time of New Kingdom, the feast of Renenutet was celebrated on the first day of this month. It is probably an old harvest festival. This is also considered the birthday of the 'corn mummy' Neper. These are small dolls made of soil mixed with grains of corn, wrapped in linen and buried each year in association with the cult of Osiris.[20]

As mentioned earlier, the festival of Rennutet was celebrated 'out of sequence' due to the transfer of an original lunar feast to the 'new' festival calendar. It was probably a full moon rite.[21]

In the Dakhleh Oasis this month was also the occasion for the major feast of Seth.

Feast of Khonsu (the wanderer)

It is strange, that during a month that from time immemorial has been dedicated to the moon god Khonsu, there is no actual record from any period of seasonal rites dedicated to his cult. Khonsu is the son of Amun and Mut, and therefore part of the Theban triad. He is shown as a mummified youth with the characteristic sidelock. He sometimes has a violent nature, see for example his appearance in the celebrated *Cannibal Hymn*:

> §393 The sky is clouded, the stars are darkened.
> The Bows move, the bones of the Earth God tremble.
> (Then all) movements cease [...]
> §397 The King is the Bull of Heaven who (once) suffered want and who has decided to live on the essence of every god, who eats their entrails when they come from the Isle of Fire with bellies full of charms. [...]
> §400 The King is he who eats men, who lives on gods, lord of messengers who gives instructions. [...]
> §402 Indeed, Khonsu (the moon), who slaughters the lords, cuts their throats for the King
> and takes out for him what is in their bellies,
> (Khonsu is) the messenger whom he sends out to chastise.[22]

A Ptolemaic text from Karnac has a version of the cosmology in which he plays a significant role. He even has a different genesis as child of crocodile god Sobek and Hathor at Kom Ombo. His associations with curses was discussed in my book *Supernatural Assault in Ancient Egypt* see *Amuletic Decrees* and *Letters to the Dead*.

Great feast of Min in Esna Calendar. Day 1

Parker thought this might originally have been new moon feast - the festival calendar at Medinet Habu, places it as day eleven which was also a new moon day, here a feast of phallic fertility god Min (Greek Pan). The feast consisted of several obscure episodes such as the 'Going forth of Min to the Stairs' - *(Prt Mnw r ht)* occurring over several days.[23]

II Shemu (Summer) - Payni - April
Day 20

In some parts of ancient Egypt, the Min festival mentioned above appears to have slipped back to this month, unless it is a completely difference feast.

The Esna festival calendar has a feast after the old 'Sed-Feast' called the 'seizing the staffs', which may be like the rites to 'Ares' witnessed by Herodotus, at an otherwise unknown location in the western delta called Papremis (or Pephremis). Elsewhere, Herodotus recalls that the Hippopotamus was the sacred animal of Papremis, which prompts many scholars to speculate that the description is of a commemoration of the conflict of Horus and Seth or Seth and Apophis, involving the theme of mother incest. Griffiths[24] argues that Ares is the Greek designation of Horus:

> At Papremis sacrifice is offered and rites performed as elsewhere; but when the sun is sinking, while a few of the

priests are left to busy themselves with the image, the greater number of them beset the entrance of the temple, with clubs of wood in their hands; they are confronted by more than a thousand men, all performing vows and all carrying wooden clubs like the rest. The image of the god, in a little wooden gilt casket, is carried on the day before this from the temple to another sacred chamber.

The few who are left with the image draw a four-wheeled cart carrying it in its casket; the other priests stand in the temple porch and prevent its entrance; the votaries take the part of the god, and smite the priests, who resist. There is hard fighting with clubs, and heads are broken, and as I think (though the Egyptians told me no life was lost), many die of their wounds. The assemblage, say the people of the country, took its rise thus:—The mother of Ares dwelt in this temple; Ares had been reared away from her, and when he grew to manhood came to have intercourse with his mother; but as her attendants, never having seen him before, kept him off and would not suffer him to pass. Ares brought men from another town, roughly handled the attendants, and gained access to his mother. From this, they say, arose this custom of a battle of blows at the festival in honour of Ares.

(Herodotus II: 63)

III Shemu (Summer) - Epiphi - May
Day 20

The occasion for the 'Beautiful Festival of the Valley'. From the 18th dynasty onwards this was one of the most famous of Egyptian feasts. Based in Thebes, it involved a procession of the cult statues of Amun, Mut & Khonsu from Karnak to Deir el Bahri just a few miles west on the opposite side of the Nile.

IV Shemu (Summer) - Mesore - June
Day 1

The feast for the hippopotamus goddess Ipet, 'her majesty' (*hmt.s*) extends over two days but from New Kingdom times was celebrated on the first day of this month..

Day 30

Mesore, the last day of the wandering year (*Arey renpet*), occurs a festive 'communion' (*mesejet*).

The Epagomenal days (herejew renpet)

Epagomenal days all have affiliations with the cult of Ra.[25] This is a five day pseudo-birthday feast. The five intercalary days between year end and year beginning, were seen since the Old Kingdom as birthdays of five gods of the Heliopolitan ennead. The text of the apoptropiac rites to accompany this dangerous twilight is as follows: [26]

The great ones are born. As for the great ones whose forms are not mysterious, beware of them. Their occasion (or, deed) will not come. . . They have proceeded.

BIRTH OF OSIRIS,

BIRTH OF HAROERIS,

BIRTH OF SETH,

BIRTH OF ISIS,

BIRTH OF NEPHTHYS.

AS TO ANYONE WHO KNOWS THE NAME OF THE FIVE EPAGOMENAL DAYS, he does not hunger, he does not thirst, Bastet does not overpower him. He will not enter into the great law court, he will not die through an enemy of the king and will not die (or, depart) through the pestilence of the year. But he will last every day (till) death arrives, whereas no illness will take possession of him.

AS TO HIM WHO KNOWS THEM, *Hw* will be prosperous within him, his speech is important to listen to in the presence of Ra.

FIRST DAY : THE BIRTH OF OSIRIS.

WORDS TO BE SAID ON IT:

O Osiris, bull in his cavern (whose) name is hidden . . . offspring (?) of his mother.

Hail to thee, hail to thee (??). I am (thy son)... O father, Osiris.

THE NAME OF THIS DAY: The pure one

SECOND DAY : THE BIRTH OF HORUS.

WORDS TO BE SAID ON IT :

O Horus, (*khenty-irty*) of Letopolis. It is repeated anew mighty of strength, master of fear, save me from bad and evil things and from any slaughter. Horus, son of Geb

THE NAME OF THIS DAY: **Powerful is the heart**

THIRD DAY : THE BIRTH OF SETH.

WORDS TO BE SAID ON IT:

OH, SETH, Son of Nut, great of strength, save me from bad and evil things and from any slaughter, protection is at thy hands of thy holiness. I am the son of thy son.

THE NAME OF THE DAY : **It is powerful of heart.**

FOURTH DAY : THE BIRTH OF ISIS.

WORDS TO BE SAID ON IT:

Oh, this Isis, daughter of Nut the eldest, mistress of magic, provider (?) of the book, mistress who appeases the two lands, her face is glorious. I am the brother and the sister.

THE NAME OF THE DAY : **He who makes terror.**

FIFTH DAY : THE BIRTH OF NEPHTHYS.

WORDS TO BE SAID ON IT :

Oh, Nephthys, daughter of Nut, sister of Seth, she whose father sees a healthy daughter, beautiful of face. Beautiful of face. I am the divine power in the womb of my mother Nut.

THE NAME OF THE DAY: **The child who is in his nest.**

WORDS TO BE SAID AFTER THEM WHEN THE EPAGOMENAL DAYS ARE COMPLETED.

Hail to you! O great ones according to their names, children of a goddess who have come forth from the sacred womb, lords because of their father, goddesses because of their mother, without knowing the necropolis. Behold, may you protect (me) and save me. May you make me prosperous, may you make protection, may you repeat and may you protect me. I am one who is on their list.

THIS SPELL IS TO BE SAID FOUR TIMES.

Make for thyself an amulet as protection, [drawn on fine linen] and placed about the neck (for the five) epagomenal days in (the name of) these gods on the day... written on the choice of... amulet... THE FEMALE FIGURE of Isis, THE FEMALE FIGURE of Nephthys... BLACK COLOUR ANOINTED WITH FIRST CLASS OIL AND FUMIGATED WITH INCENSE ON A BURNER. THEY SHOULD BE PURIFIED, LOOSENED, AND THROWN INTO WATER for the father Nun and for the mother Nut after the day of the birth of Ra and act. Behold, make for thyself a big 3^cbt of bread, beer, oxen, fowl, carob beans incense *ty-sps-wood* and all kinds of dates and vegetables — being clean, being clean in front of Ra-Harakhti when he shines in the eastern horizon of heaven and when he sets in the western horizon. Behold, thou bathest in the fresh water ... of the beginning of inundation. Paint thine eyes with green paint; take a drink of wine and anoint thyself...

Notes

1. Redford, D B (2001) *Oxford Encyclopedia of Ancient Egypt* - 'Work'
2. Numbers 1 & 10 (*mdw*) are (Z1) & (V20) respectively in Gardiner's sign list. See Simpson, W K, *Papyrus Reisner*, 5 vols. See also Kadish, G E (1996) 'Observations on Time and Work discipline in Ancient Egypt.' in *Studies in honour of W Kelly Simpson* ed by Manuelian, P Der and R Freed. 2 vols Boston.
3. Nilsson, Martin P (1920) *Primitive Time Reckoning*, Lund : 171

There is an Arab grouping of nights into threes -

1-3	bright ones
4.6	overlapping nights
7-9	the nine
10-12	The ten
13 - 15	the white ones
16 - 18	the white ones with black heads (moon rises after dark)
19-21	dark nights
22-24	very dark nights
25-27	da'adi (uncertain meaning)
28-30	to extinguish

4. Nilsson 1920 : 171
5. Nilsson 1920 : 77
6. Morgan, C (2002) *Medicine of the Gods: basic principles of Ayurvedic medicine,* Mandrake.
7. Depuydt, L (1997) *Civil Calendar and Lunar Calendar in Ancient Egypt,* Leuven. : 130
8. Depuydt (op cit) calls this the 'Brugsch phenomenon' whereby the last month is named as if it is the first. The phenomena is generated by the relationship between lunar and civil calendars. Added to this we have the so-called 'Gardiner phenomenon' (named after the famous Egyptologist Alan Gardiner). Existing texts show that the festivals were not celebrated in the appropriate month but seem to have shifted backwards. Hence the Egyptian month Mesore 'Birth of Ra' occurs in the twelfth month of the year. Gardiner's theory was that Mesore was originally the first month of the year - although the phenomenon he is trying to explain might alternatively be caused by the transfer of feasts from a lunar to a civil year which was the solution of his contemporary Richard Parker's (1957 : 57), with which Gardiner strongly disagreed.
9. 'Wag-Fest' in *Lexicon*

10. Spalinger, A (1993) 'A chronological analysis of the feast of *thy*' *Studien Zur Altägyptischer Culture* 20, pp289-303. See also Nilsson (1920) for further data on the significance of number 19.
11. Other parallels include the myth of Onuris and Mehit.
12. Gardiner, A H (1935) *Hieratic Papyri in the British Museum (HPIBM) series III* vol 1 text of Dream Book
13. Bakir, A M, (1960) *The Cairo Calendar*, An Almanac of Lucky & Unlucky Days.
14. Spalinger (1993) Assume there was a year when the old lunar and the new civil calendar ran side by side for one last time; assume a year when the civil calendar was inaugurated - the old lunar years completed its twelve month cycle in 254 days. The new civil version still has a further eleven days to run, by which time the lunar year would have started another lunar month of 30 days, which finally ends (ie new moon) on twentieth day of the first civil month. Does this give us a clue to other feasts set on or around the twentieth day that they were originally new moon feasts? And does this mean that the old month of *Thy* was actually the second month - the first falling under the auspices of Ra?

    For more evidence for a lunar Wag feast see Posener-Kriéger (1985) excavation at Abusir which confirmed Parker's thesis. There is also the problem of the double dating of some festivals eg: The Illahun papyris reveals that the Wag feast was celebrated on the fixed date of 1 Akhet 18 (ie 18th day of the first month). The eminent scholar Borchardt also found 'moveable' dates for this occuring in the tenth month. There was also a moveable Wag feast. The scholar Spalinger has collated all the dates and finds that months 3-8 and 12 all have lunar doubles or partners ie a feast that took place on the first day following the month that should have contained them.
15. 'Opet' in *Lexicon*
16. Shaw I & Paul Nicholson (1995) 'Hathor'
17. 'Choiak' in *Lexicon*

Parker 1950 : 59sq. The calendar of Edfu has the following entry after Choiak 28: "The feast 21 of iht hr hiwt (the fifth lunar day). Performing his rites." If Choiak 28 is the fifth lunar day, then Choiak 24 is *psdntyw*. If we refer this to the Dendera text, the underlying symbolism is immediately apparent.

18. The better known version of the Osiris myth has, to be sure, his embalmment on the 24th; but his burial does not take place until the 30th. It is not my intention to pursue this fascinating topic any further in these pages. It is clear, however, that, while the relation between Osiris and the moon has been known for some time, not all the ramifications of this relationship have as yet been explored. Nor has the connection between Horus and the moon been suspected.

19. Shorter, Alan W (1935), 'The God Nehebkau', *JEA* XXi pp47sq

20. M J Raven, 'Corn Mummies' *OMRO* 63 (1982) 7.38

21. Parker, Richard A (1950) *The Calendars of Ancient Egypt*, Chicago : 249

22. For Cannibal Hymn see PT ; 'Chons' in *Lexikon;* Quirke, Stephen (1992) *Ancient Egyptian Religion*; Lesko L (1991) 'Ancient Egyptian Cosmogonies and Cosmology' in Shafer, Byron (1991) *Religion in Ancient Egypt* pp103-107; Lesko L & Richard Parker (1988) 'The Khonsu Cosmology' in *Pyramid Studies and other essays presented to I E S Edwards*, edited by John Baines pp 168-175.

23. Parker (1950). Grimm (1994) 435-41 has refuted Parker's Ptolemaic evidence concerning the feast of Min.

24. Griffiths, J G (1960) *The Conflict of Horus and Seth*, Liverpool p85sq

25. Wells, R A 1994 'Re and the Calendars' in Spalinger 1994 (ed.) in *Revolutions in Time: Studies in Ancient Egyptian Calendars*, Van Siclen, Texas. fn 83

26. Bakir, A M, (1960) *Cairo Calendar* or *Almanac of Lucky and Unlucky Days*.

3 The lunar-stellar calendar of Horus & Set

A feast for the first night of the Prophet and his Bride!
A feast for the three of the writing of the Book of the Law.
A feast for Tahuti and the child of the Prophet
-- secret, O Prophet!
A feast for the Supreme Ritual,
and a feast for the Equinox of the Gods.
A feast for fire and a feast for water;
a feast for life and a greater feast for death!
A feast every day in your hearts in the joy of my rapture!
A feast every night unto Nu,
and the pleasure of uttermost delight!
The Book of the Law (Crowley) II. 37-43

In the last chapter, I presented a paradigm of the Ancient Egyptian festival year. It is now universally accepted that as measurements of time, the day and the lunar month come before the concept of the year. In other words the very oldest Egyptian ritual calendar was lunar, but is now lost. I want to try and reconstruct that lost lunar calendar. I want to present the ancient Egyptian religious year as it was practiced in the very ancient times, when cultures such as those described in *The Bull of Ombos* were the norm. That is to say before the unification of Egypt circa 3100BCE, before the hegemony of the cult of Horus and Osiris; when strange savage gods such as Seth were in their prime. It goes without saying that I personally think a reconstruction of the old

Sethian point of view, has something of abiding value to the modern pagan sensibility currently in construction.

The Lunar Calendar

The evidence for this is speculative and very complex. In the words of Leo Depuydt, it does not exactly jump out at you, whereas the existence of the well known Egyptian civil calendar is beyond doubt.

Alongside the predominant civil calendar discussed above, several other calendars continued a parallel if more veiled existence. There is also strong evidence for a 'secret' lunar calendar, in partial use by the priesthood to determine the dates of one or two festivals, which unlike most others, really could not ignore their lunar roots. See for example my comments on the lunar feast of *Wag* in previous chapter.

The best evidence for priestly use of a lunar calendar comes from records at Illahun or El Lahun, situated where Bahr Yusuf enters the Fayum. The place is known for the Kahun Papyri, many hundred of Hieratic texts - mathematical, medical, veterinary, and administrative documents. Among them, are shift rosters for the cohorts of priests who staffed the Fayum's many temples. Egypt had very few permanent priests - most eligible men (and some women)[1] served the temple in rotation. A priest's tour of duty was measured in lunar months.

What I want to do in this chapter is lay before you the evidence of the original, archaic version of that lunar calendar, before it was occulted into the hands of the priesthood. This is a much more speculative venture, and relies on the interpretation of some very obscure evidence, the deconstruction of textual sources, and a measure of inspired guesswork. Although this evidence is obscure, requiring some quite technical argument, that does not mean it is weak. Thus some popular authors may be forgiven for failing to notice its existence. It all hinges around the reading of some so-called double-dated inscriptions. The first example was identified by the pioneer of Egyptian calendar studies, Heinrich Brugsch, who in 1872 published the first known example of a double date. It concerns the date of a famous battle of Megiddo, in which Thutmose III waged war against the Syro-Palestinian city of Qadesh:

> In year 23 (of the reign of Thutmosis III), (civil day) I Shemu 21 (21st day of the first month of the harvest season), the day of the feast of Pesedjenet exactly (i.e: New Moon Day).[2]

There are about eight similar examples of where a day in the Egyptian civil calendar is supplemented by a reference to a lunar event - thus implying that another lunar calendar was in operation 'behind the scenes'.

It might be that the use of the lunar calendar was so familiar, that it was never written down. You might recall how the Egyptian had names for each month - for example 'Mesore' (IV Shemu) but these occur in very few inscriptions. Every native Egyptian just knew the name as we know that 1/1 is 1st of January.[3]

The eight known double dates (more if you include other more ambiguous examples) probably refer to days of special importance in the month. These are:

Day 1	new moon	(*pesedenetew*)
Day 5	offerings on the altar	(*jehet her hawet*)
Day 6	sixth day feast	(*senewet*)
Day 15	full moon day	(*semedet*)
Day 16	second arrival	(*meseper senenew*)
Day 23	second quarter day	(*denejet senenew*)

The temple rosters of Illahun listed

Day 1	new moon	(*pesedenetew*)
Day 2	first crescent	(*tep 3bed*)
Day 4	Going forth of Sem priests	(*peret sem*)
Day 6	sixth day feast	(*senewet*)
Day 15	full moon	(*semedet*)

Dates such as the above form part of a lunar year that shadowed the civil year, and was therefore only of secondary importance. This is similar to the manner in which our own observations of the moon are dependent upon the familiar Gregorian calendar.

The priests of Illahun were hardly addicted to moon watching. Like everyone else their focus was mainly on the civil calendar. A single priest, the so-called 'overseer of the hour' (*imeyew wenwet*)[4] was attached to each temple House of Life. It was his job to say when the new 'temple' month should start. This he did by observation of the waning moon. Each night he looked for it in the sky. When it was invisible, day one of the cycle began in the morning. The lunar month had no special name but was simply (and for us confusingly) named after the civil month in which it started.

If you think about it, the special priest could have done his 'little' task just once in the year, leaving everything else to be named in sequence. The technical name for this is 'yearly pairing'. But most scholars now think the task was done every month, so-called 'monthly pairing' - each month individually named. No one knows what happened if there was more than one new moon in any month - a so-called Blue moon, or second conjunction. If you are interested in some historical background as to how other cultures coped with these sort of issues, the standard work is still Martin Nilsson's *Primitive Time Reckoning*.

Sirius & the Lunar-Stellar Calendar

So far the discussion has been about a lunar calendar, clearly subordinated to the ancient Egyptian civil based year. Now, I want to turn to the Sirius based system, whose existence has gradually emerged in the work of several scholars.[5]

The great pioneer in this field was Heinrich Brugsch, closely followed by Ludwig Borchardt. Their work was brought to a wider audience by Richard Parker, a professor at Brown University, Rhode Island, who wrote in English. All three men focused on a tiny informal calendar written on back of the beginning of a medical manuscript - the so-called Papyrus Ebers.

The Papyrus Ebers was bought from an Arab dealer in Luxor by Egyptologist George Ebers (1837-1898). It contains over a hundred columns of prescriptions, covering around 45 different classes of disease. It is normally paired up with the *Edwin Smith Surgical Papyrus*. Time has always been an important aspect of medicine. Ancient medical systems use a great many herbs in their medicaments, and these are often to be gathered by what we nowadays call 'bio-dynamic' principles, that is to say by observation of the sun and moon. So for example the potency of fresh herbs is likely to be greater if they are picked by moon light. Medical calendars are therefore strongly lunar. It's extremely likely that medical practitioners were another group that relied upon an observational lunar calendar well after it was superceeded in other walks of life, by the civil version. And sure enough, the reverse side of the *Papyrus Ebers* contains a little calendar with huge implications. **Figure 15** is a transcription of the hieroglyphs, followed in **Table 4** with its transliteration and partial translation:

Since the discovery of the Ebers calendar a great deal of ink has been expended on its analysis. The only thing we need focus on here, is the list of names in the righthand or first column. Could this be a version of an original lunar calendar? Many scholars have thought so, starting with Borchardt and most recently with Leo Depuydt, a leading expert on the Egyptian language. For Depuydt the most plausible explanation for the difference beween 'theophoric' month names in Ebers, and the later civil calendar, is that it refers to an older tradition probably an original lunar calendar.[6] In **Table 4** I have isolated the month names:

Figure 15: Hieroglyphic transcription of Ebers calendar from Parker, Richard A (1950) *The Calendars of Ancient Egypt*, Chicago.

Table 4: The Calendar of Medical Papyrus Ebers		
3	2	1
Year 9 under the majesty of the King of Upper and Lower Egypt, *dsr-k3-r'* (Amenhotep I) may he live forever		
heliacal rising of Sothis	iii shemu 9	*wp-rnpt*
ditto	iv shemu 9	*thy*
ditto	i akhet 9	*mnh*
ditto	ii akhet 9	*Hwt-hr*
ditto	iii akhet 9	*k3 hr k3*
ditto	iv akhet 9	*šf bdt*
ditto	i peret 9	*rkh wr*
ditto	ii peret 9	*rkh ndš*
ditto	iii peret 9	*Rnwtt*
ditto	iv peret 9	*Hnśw*
ditto	i shemu 9	*Hnt-hty*
ditto	ii shemu 9	*jpt hmt*

Table 4: The Calendar of Medical Papyrus Ebers

Some important differences emerge straight away. For instance, the goddess Hathor seems to have been celebrated a month earlier in II Akhet, instead of the more familiar III Akhet in the civil calendar. This time lag between the civil calendar and lunar calendar could be explained by the transfer forward in time from one calendar to another.[7]

It has to be said that there could be other explanations for the difference. Firstly, it assumes that the names in the Ebers calendar are of the whole month, and not some feast occuring in that month. In addition you need to bear in mind that ancient Egypt had many regional variations in terms of cult symbolism and religious practice. Some popular books on Egypt tend to ignore this fact, and subsume all Egyptian religion into one monolithic cult that is supposed to have existed at all times and places. It is true that some cults were more popular than others. Some, such as that of Osiris, had a national, even international manifestation. Whereas others, such as Ipet, the Hippopotamus goddess, sustained on a very local base at Oxyrhynchus. Even so, for many, the local was more immediate than the national, in the same way that once upon a time in the west, a local saint, St Frideswide, although part of the overall Christian scheme of things, had a special place in the heart of Oxford's citizens.

On this issue, Kaper's recent study of an astronomical ceiling from the sanctuary of a 1st or 2nd century temple at Deir el Haggar is very revealing.[8] Deir el Haggar is in the Dakhleh Oasis, more than 400^{km} west of the Nile, in the Western Desert. Dakhleh conserves many unique religious forms because of its isolation.

Dakhleh was a cult centre for the worship of Seth. Evidence from the astronomical ceiling indicates the importance of lunar symbolism and timing to their rites. They closely followed the ebb and flow of the lunar currents, which were allegorized as the opposition of the sun and moon. The 'white nights' were especially important, that is to say the full moon and the days leading up and immediately after. This 3.25m x 2.42m astronomical ceiling has four registers of information including a lunar calendar of yearly feasts elsewhere abandoned. The gods of these feasts represent a specifically local tradition heavily influenced by the cult of Seth. The ritual year for the residents of Dakhleh began with an explicit adoration of Hathor, who usually has to wait until the third month to get some refreshment. Next, they celebrated the cult of Ipet the Hippopotamus goddess, and in their third month they celebrated a god totally unknown outside the desert areas - the 'typhonian' god Tutu. Evidence from the so-called *Dakhleh stele* also indicated the local importance of Hathor and Seth, the later feasted on the 25th day of the eighth month (Pharmuthi) which we can surmise fell on or near the full moon. From the people of Dakhleh we also learn of the four cosmic winds that mark the cardinal directions. They have their origin in the body of Nuit and are commanded by the god Shu.

The people of Dakhleh were seriously 'out of step' with the dominant civil calendar that had existed from the time of the writing of the Pyramid Texts and continued in use throughout Egypt's long history. The people of Dakhleh conserved an archaic lunar year based on intuition and observation that informed opinion says only existed in Egypt's dim and distant past. For most Egyptians,

| Table 5: Month names of medical Papyrus Ebers |||||
A	B	C	D	E
		Transliteration & possible meaning	Associated deity	
1	wp-rnpt	opener of the year	Ra	iii Shemu (harvest)
2	thy	Tekhy - cup 'feast of drunkenness		iv Shemu
3	mnht	menekhet	Min	i Akhet (inundation)
4	Hwt-hr	Hathor	Hathor	ii Akhet
5	k3 hr k3	ka hor ka 'joining of kas'	Sokar / Osiris	iii Akhet
6	šf bdt	Shef bedet 'swelling of emmer wheat'		iv Akhet
7	rkh wr	Rekh wer 'greater burning' ie: cold season		i Peret (planting)
8	rkh ndš	rekh nedjes 'lesser burning'		ii Peret
9	Rnwtt	Renenutet	Renenutet	iii Peret
10	Hnśw	Khonsu	Khonsu	iv Peret
11	Hnt-hty	Khenty-khety	Horus	i Shemu (harvest)
12	jpt hmt	Ipet hemet	Ipet	ii Shemu

Table 5: The Calendar of Medical Papyrus Ebers with details of month names

this older lunar-stellar calendar ran alongside the new civil version, until it was completely replaced most likely in 1320BCE (when the Sothic cycle was in synchronization with the civil year).

This Lunar calendar is the essential key to Egyptian religion. Even so, it is routinely ignored in what are otherwise quite reasonable sources, for example Sherif El Sabbai's *Temple Festivals & Calendars of Ancient Egypt*[9] raises and then dismisses in a few lines the provision for regular monthly lunar feasts, concluding that 'these appear to be of secondary importance and were celebrated during daylight hours.' Sabbai was perhaps unaware of more recent research on the significance of the morning penumbra and twilight in ancient Egyptian ritual. Indeed, the original meaning of *duat*, usually translated as the 'otherworld', is according to Gardiner, the 'early morning twilight'.[10]

How did the lunar calendar work?

As you probably know, when the sun and moon line up in the same part of the ecliptic, it is known in astronomy as a conjunction, and in common parlance as the new moon. Lunar calendars are always based on the period between one conjunction and the next, the so-called 'synodic' month. Because the moon has an elliptical orbit – it changes speed depending on its proximity to the earth – the synodic month varies between 29.26 and 29.80 days.

Likewise the visibility of the old and new crescent varies in proportion to its latitude and 'anomaly' - for example, it is easier to see the crescent at Babylon than it is at Stonehenge.

If it weren't for these irregularities, then each lunar month would alternate between 29 and 30 days. However, in the real world several 30 day synodic months in succession is quite possible. In addition to these natural 'irregularities' the observation of lunar cycles is subject to 'observer error'. For one reason or another, the old and new crescent may be unobserved or occulted when theoretically it should be visible.

For reasons such as the above, the apparent motion can be quicker in the first half of the month than it is in the second. Therefore, the half month also varies between 13.73 and 15.80 days.

The Lunar month

The ancient Egyptian day began at dawn.[11] The day and lunar month begin at the same time. The way they determined the first day of the month differs from many other ancient cultures with two notable exceptions – the Massai & the Loango of East Africa. The similarities may indicate Egyptian influence or perhaps African influence on ancient Egypt.

It is now widely accepted that the first day began on the morning after the final disappearance of the old crescent, i.e. when it is no longer visible in the eastern sky before sunrise.[12] This is an observation that requires no special skill and is as valid now as it was during ancient times. The only requirement being that you miss a few nights sleep during the final days of the waning moon.

Now you might be saying to yourself "I can just look that up in an ephemeris or read it in the newspapers". All this is true, but it is good to remind yourself that the conjunction is an *invisible* event known nowadays by inference. It is not such a bad idea to consider how you would determine this without all the conveniences of modern life. The observer needs to watch the moon carefully each night as the moon wanes digit by digit. If the crescent is no longer visible during a particular evening, when the sun rises it will be the first day of a new lunar month.

Almost all cultures have a name or symbol for this day. In the language of the ancient Egyptians, it is known as *pese̱denet* (new moon). The names of the other thirty days of the month were first identified by Heinrich Brugsch in his 1883 Thesaurus.[13] We have already encountered some of these names in our earlier discussion on double dates (see above) **Table 6** reproduces the entire set.

The Lunar Year

In the previous section, we discovered how to set the first day of the month. Now we determine the first lunar month of the yearly cycle. How does it all begin?

So far in this book, I have referred to an original lunar calendar existing before the Egyptian dynasties. This was a thesis first advanced by Richard Parker in his groundbreaking monograph *The Calendars of Ancient Egypt*.[14] Recent research has refined this view, and identified that there were in fact at least two lunar calendars operating in pre-dynastic Egypt - one based in the north and the other in the south.[15]

Table 6: Ancient Egyptian Lunar Days - Light Half			
Lunar phase	Egyptian name (vocalic 'e' added for ease of reading)	Translation	Notes
1	pesedeteyw		
2	tep 3bed	new crescent day	
3	meseper	arrival day	
4	prt sem	day of going forth of the Sem priest	
5	3het h3t	day of offerings on the altar	
6	senet	sixth day	
7	den3t	part day, first quarter day	
8	tep		
9	k3p		
10	sif		
11	setet		
12			
13	m33 sty		
14	si3w		
15	semedet	half-moon day, full moon	

Table 6: Names of the Lunar Days (from Heinrich Brugsch's *Thesaurus Inscriptionum Aegyptiacarum*)

Table 6: Ancient Egyptian Lunar Days - Light Half			
Lunar day	Egyptian name (vocalic 'e' added for ease of reading)	Translation	Notes
16	mešeper šen-new	second arrival day	
17	šȝw		
18	iʿh	day of the moon	
19	šedem medew.ef		
20	šetep		
21	ʿperew		
22	ph ʿsepedet		
23	denit	part day, last quarter day	
24	kenehw		
25	šetet		
26	peret		
27	wŠb		
28	heb-šed newet	day of the going forth of Nuit	
29	ʿhȝ		
30	peret Min	day of the going forth of Min	

The northern version, centred around Heliopolis, was regulated by the 'Birth of Ra' at the winter solstice. The Southern version, centred around the predynastic culture of Nagada, was regulated by the Heliacal rising of Sirius, which occurred close to the Summer Solstice. The genesis of this predynastic Lunar-Sothic calendar is estimated to be 5000-4500BCE. It was then that the rising of Sirius and the Nile would be historically closest. That southern or Upper Egypt was the locus for the Sirius based lunar calendar is underlined by the presence of a cult of Sirius at Egypt's frontier settlement at Elephantine. Elephantine, situated at the first cataract of the Nile, was considered to be the place where the Nile was born. This important regional centre has a ritual complex with a newly discovered shrine of the goddess Satet - the personification of Sirius.[16] The goddess Satet was identified with Sothis for at least 3000 years up to the Ptolemaic times. The Sirius orientation is present in one of the doorways to the principal room of this shrine.

The attentive reader will have noticed that northern and southern calendars each have conflicting start dates. The eventual syncretisation of both these calendars, is another possible explanation for the 'problems' in later Egyptian month names eg: that the month name 'Mesore - Birth of Re' is the twelfth month, when its name would implies a beginning and therefore first month position. More of this below - for an examination of the Nagada culture see my *Bull of Ombos*.[17]

The Northern Lunar-Solar calendar

In the north, in Egypt's Nile delta region, observations would probably have focussed on the Sun god's apparent 'journey' south and his eventual return. The journey is quite subtle, and involves observations of variations of the point at which the sun breaks over the horizon at dawn. It is the kind of observation that might be facilitated by structures such as the familiar stone and wooden henges of Neolithic Europe. Try it next time you are there at dawn. At the summer solstice, the sun is at its most northerly rising point. In Egypt this will be north-eastern N65°E. Over the coming days and months it makes the journey 'south' to its most southerly rising point at the winter solstice north-eastern N118°E.

It is not very well known that a number of Egyptian temples have winter sunrise orientations - one of the best examples is the temple of Hatshepsut at Deir el Bahri. This temple often crops up in matters of astro-archeology. Very few temples have summer solstice orientation.

The *Book of Gates* is an ancient Egyptian text found in various locations including the coffin of Sety I, currently displayed in the John Soanes Museum in London.[18] In astro-archeology, this text is viewed as an ancient Egyptian primer in the art of telling the time at night. The obscure deity names found in this kind of text are probably some sort of star clock. So for instance, the caverns of the *Duat,* parallel the invisible portions of Nuit's body through the year.[19] Thus, several bright stars needed to be selected in order to form the star-clock. Observations are easier if several attendant stars point to and herald the principal star marker. So for example,

Sothis, is 'heralded' by several stars in the Orion constellation - the triangle being: Betelgeuse, Rigel and then Sirius. These kind of observations are very like those described earlier in connection with the use of the moon's last crescent to determine the first day of the lunar month. A great many important events in ancient Egypt were determined by observations of the heliacal rising of stars and planets. If you want to be like the ancient Egyptians, you have to be an early riser!

The sun god Ra's astrological journey is mirrored in Egyptian mythology. He is born at the winter solstice, and enters the underworld - the *duat* at the vernal equinox. During the hours of night he continues to travel and gestate there for the nine months (272 days) until, the following winter solstice, when he is again reborn. This mythology was underpinned by observations of the night sky, and especially the Milky Way. The Egyptians viewed the Milky Way as the body of the star goddess Nuit.

Richard Wells made the following interesting discovery:

> 'It so happens that the outer arm of our galaxy, a band of myriads of stars called the Milky Way, when seen in its entirety over the course of a year has the appearance of a female shrouded in the thinnest of gauze robes (see illustration). The Milky Way bifurcates into two appendages at the constellation of Cygnus forming the legs of the anthropomorphic body. Further along, the star clouds swell in the vicinity of Gemini to form the head with even the suggestion of the cloth headdress, hanging down the back.'[20]

Ra enters the *duat* at sunset on the spring equinox. In terms of the cycle of the year, this could be considered as the god's conception. We can assume that our Egyptian ancestors marked the exact point at which the sun set on the horizon, by using a convenient landmark. If you were to look to that point in the west, an hour or two after sunset, when the sky is dark enough for you to see the Milky Way, you might observe an interesting phenomenon. The part of the Milky Way above identified as the head and especially the 'mouth' of Nuit, is over precisely the same spot. It is as if Nuit has just eaten the sun, which is in fact how this mystery is expressed in Egyptian mythology. As an aside, I would add that there are echoes of the above process in Egyptian physiology, and what we might call its 'body magick'. Body magick is a generic term for the kind of secret techniques that are more

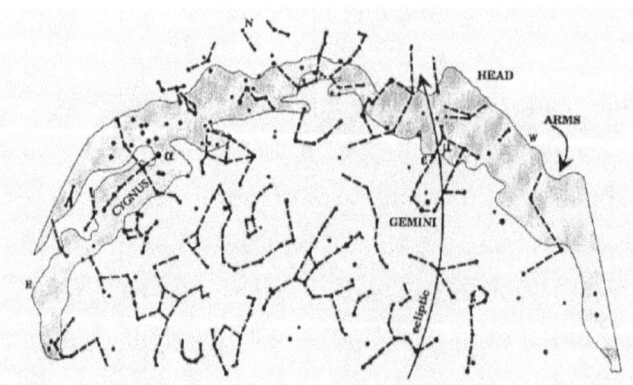

Figure 16: The stars of the Milky Way and their relationship to the star goddess Nuit.

familiar in later times, or as it is more often called Hindu and Buddhist Tantrism. The Birth of Ra occurs 272 days after conception on the morning of the winter solstice. This period of gestation is the same for us lesser mortals. Rather amazingly the Birth of Ra also has a stellar component. The winter sun rises against a backdrop of the constellation Cygnus, whose star 'Y' corresponds with the 'yoni' or birth canal of Nuit.

The Lunar-Stellar or Lunar-Sothic Calendar

> In the first month, on the fourteen day of the month in the evening is the lord's passover. And on the fifteen day of the same month is the feast of the unleavened bread to the Lord; seven days you shall eat unleavened bread.
>
> Leviticus 23:5-6

We turn then to the southern version of the ancient Egyptian lunar year governed by the heliacal rising of Sirius. Its use centred around the predynastic culture of Nagada, its genesis estimated to be 5000-4500BCE.

Every star has one conjunction with the sun every year. During this time, they are invisible to the earthly observer. This period of invisibility depends on the distance from the ecliptic, but for Sirius, the brightest of stars, its period of invisibility is approximately 70 days.

According to the Julian calendar, the Heliacal Rising of Sirius occurs around 17/19th July. As is well known, July is also the month of the annual Nile inundation, although like any natural phenomena, it is sometimes a day or two early or late, and sometimes it fails altogether. These irregularities make it unlikely that it was the origin of a 365 day year.[21]

Theoretically the heliacal rising of Sirius should occur near to the first day of the first month of the year. However, because the Egyptians allowed their civil year to 'wander' both dates rarely coincided. Those occasions when they did was often utilized for some calendar reform. For example the introduction of the Julian calendar into Egypt, occurred at a time when the heliacal rising of Sirius, and the month I Akhet were in syncronisation.[22]

The heliacal rising of Sirius was known to the ancient Egyptians as *peret sepedet* - 'the going forth of Sothis', which was synonymous in later times with the phrase *wep renpet* - 'the opener of the year'. You have to ask yourself how the people of ancient Nagada co-ordinated the rising of this star with the waxing and waning of the moon? For example, did the lunar year begin the morning immediately following the heliacal rising - the so-called Solar-Sothic year? Or did the year start on the next new moon after the heliacal rising - the so-called Lunar-Sothic year?

What happened if there was still several days of the old lunar year still to go? In practice, the difference could be anything short of an entire lunar month. In other words, what happened if the moon was a clear but still waning crescent in the night sky? That is one of the key questions in calibrating a strictly lunar calendar.

The solution to this issue was probably as follows:

The lunar year began with the first new moon immediate after the heliacal rising of Sothis.

You might want to refer to the section above to remind yourself how to determine the new moon. If the new moon occurs within less than 11 days of the heliacal rising of Sirius there needs to be an intercalary or thirteenth lunar month to make up the difference.

Parker thought this extra month, occurring approximately every three years, was dedicated to Thoth. Depuydt, an expert on the Egyptian language reminds us of the fact that the month that occurs at the end of the sequence shares something with the beginning of the next year. Thus, he calls it a 'straddle' month. It might remind you of the contemporary Christian calendar, which is a celebration of birth that nonetheless occurs in the twelfth month when its natural position should be in the first.[23]

Egyptian month names share some of this ambiguity. In the lunar calendars known of from other cultures, intercalary or straddle months have no unique name, but merely repeat the name of either the last or occasional the first month of the year. For example, in the Jewish calendar, which is also lunar, we can find a second century account of Gamaliel II, one of the three learned Rabbi's charged with the task of keeping the calendar in tune with the seasons. He writes:

> 'We make known to you that the lambs are small and the young of the birds are tender and the time of the corn harvest has not come, so that it seems right to me and my brothers to add to this year thirty days.' [24]

The Jews usually added a final month Adar II or sometimes used the first month - Nisan II. It seems likely that the Egyptians had a similar system, repeating one of their month names where needed, approximately every three years. Thus, the straddle month has various names including: *wep renpet* : 'opener of the year' and Ra Horakhty: 'Horus of the two horizons'.

In the archaic lunar calendar, the subsequent months were then named after whichever god's feast actually fell in that month. The mortuary temple of Rameses II (1279-1213BCE) has what is usually considered to be a technically superior version of the lunar calendar. The feasts described in Chapter 1 are based mostly on the above with some information from the Senmut version in his tomb (TT353) near the Temple of Hatshepsut at Deir el-Bahri.[25]

The Babylonian lunar calendar avoided 'leap years' by using a nineteen year cycle which, plotted all 235 lunations over the period -12 years of 12 lunar months, interspersed with 7 years of 13 lunar months. It is possible that the Egyptians attempted something similar in the Carlsberg Papyrus which has a 25 year cycle - 16 years of 12 lunar months, and 9 years of 13 lunar months. Whether the speculations of the Carlsberg Papyrus were ever used is thought unlikely by most experts in this field.

In the original lunar-stellar calendar the first fixed month 'Tekhen' was an Egyptian New Year feast of 'drunkenness'. Whoever invented the later festival calendar, replaced Tekhen with the name Djhuty or Thoth. There is a theory that Thoth's name had previously been reserved for the occasional extra or intercalary thirteenth lunar month that was to be added to the cycle every third year.

Notes & References

1. Shaw, Ian (1995) *Dictionary of Ancient Egypt*, BM. 'priest'

2. Parker R (1950 : 29) *The Calendars of Ancient Egypt*, Chicago; Depuytd, L (1997) *Civil Calendar and Lunar Calendar in Ancient Egypt*, Leuven; for analysis of all available double dates. See also Faulkner (1942) 'The Battle of Megiddo' JEA XXVIII, 4, 11.

3. The following is a rare example from the Almanac of Lucky & Unlucky Days that does list the seasonal month names alongside their individual names:

I. akhet : Hours of Daylight,	16 Hours of Darkness,	8
II. akhet: ,, ,,14 ,, ,,	10	Phaophi.
III akhet: ,, ,,12 ,, ,,	12	Athyr.
IV. akhet: ,, ,,10 ,, ,,	14	Khoiak.
I. peret: ,, ,,8	,, ,, 16	Tybi.
II. peret: ,, ,,6	,, ,, 18	Mekhir.
III. peret: ,, ,,8	,, ,, 16	Phamenoth.
IV. peret: " "	10 " " 14	Pharmuthi.
I. shomu: ,, ,,12	,, ,, 12	Pakhons.
II shomu: ,, ,,	12 (sic.) ,, ,, (blank)	Payni
III. shomu: ,, ,,	16 ,, ,, 8	Epeiph.
IV. shomu: (blank)	18 ,, ,, 6	Wp-mpt

4. Well R A (1994) 'Re & the Calendars' in Spalinger (1994) *Revolutions in Time: Studies in Ancient Egyptian Calendars*

5. Depuydt 1997 : 208

6. Depuydt 1997 : 229

7. Depuydt 1997 : 214

8. Kaper (1995) 'The Astronomical Ceiling of Deir el Haggar in the Dakhleh Oasis' *JEA* 81 pp.151-73. For the 'Dakhleh Stele' see also Gardiner, A H (1933) *JEA* pp. 19-33. For

information on Seth worship in Dakhleh see Osing (1985) *MDAIK* 41, 229-33.

9. El Sabbai, S (2000) *Temple Festivals & Calendars of Ancient Egypt*, Liverpool.

10. See N14 in Gardiner's *Egyptian Grammar* sign list.

11. Our own term 'day' signifies a single unit of night and day; although actually our modern day begins at midnight. The word is thus a survival from older times when the day did literally begin at dawn or with the new day.

12. Parker (1950) Chapter 1

13. Brugsch, Heinrich (1883) *Thesaurus Inscriptionum Aegyptiacarum*, 6 vols Leipzig. : 46-48.

14. Parker (1950)

15. Wells, RA 1994 'Re and the Calendars' in Spalinger (1994) (ed.) in *Revolutions in Time: Studies in Ancient Egyptian Calendars*, Van Siclen, Texas.

16. Wells (1994) . Footnote 8 for more details. Wells 1986 *SAK*, 12 274 -275.

17. Morgan, M (2006) *The Bull of Ombos: Seth and Egyptian magick II*, Mandrake.

18. Sharp, S (1864) *The Alabaster Sarcophagus of Oimenpthah I (Sety I) in John Soanes Museum*, London

19. Wells, RA (1994) 'Re and the Calendars' in Spalinger, A J (1994) (ed.) in *Revolutions in Time: Studies in Ancient Egyptian Calendars*, Van Siclen, Texas. : 10

20. Wells, RA (1994) 'Re and the Calendars' in Spalinger (1994) (ed.) in *Revolutions in Time: Studies in Ancient Egyptian Calendars*, Van Siclen, Texas.

21. Nilsson uses the term 'pars pro toto' - the part stands for the whole this kind of observation

22. Depuydt (1997: 17)

23. See thirteen moons of the European tradition.

    Cycle starts again with new moon after winter solstice - if extra needed use Ice moon

    Long Night; Ice; Snow; Death

    Awakening; Grass; Planting; Rose

    Lightning; Harvest; Hunter's; Falling Leaf; Tree.

24. Quoted in Nilsson (1920 : 245). According to Nilsson the ancient Hebrews adopted the indigenous 'Canaanite' versions of month names, abandoning, assuming they ever knew them, the Egyptian versions; although they continued to share the word Yaeh - 'Full Moon'.

25. See Parker (1950 : 42) - 'In the first column of the Ebers calendar the last month of the year appears at the head of the months merely because its eponymous feast determined the following year.

4 Deities attending the Northern Constellations - the lunar days

'The belief in the existence of a lunar calendar in Egypt before the civil calendar was until recently based almost exclusively on analogy with other primitive peoples and on passages, frequently obscure, in classical writings.' [1]

'I shall keep you safe from the gods of the months of the Inundation. I shall keep you safe from the gods of the months of Winter. I shall keep you safe from the gods of the months of Harvest... I shall keep you safe from the gods of the book "That which is in the year".' [2]

Senmut was the Vizier and possible lover of Dowager Queen Hatshepsut (1503-1482BCE). Senmut's unfinished tomb at Deir el-Bahri, just across the river from modern Luxor, contains not just the finest, but also Egypt's oldest intact astronomical ceiling.

The northern half of this intensely complex glyph was reproduced in *The Bull of Ombos*.[3] Despite its great age, it points even further back into the mists of Egyptian culture, to the pre-dynastic times, when the moon played a much more significant role. The eminent scholar Richard Parker, building on the work of Heinrich Brugsch and Ludwig Borchardt, was the first to recognize the existence of what he called the original lunar calendar. This science of the moon was known and used by all people before the unification of Egypt c3100BCE – and before the creation of the civil calendar by the Amun priesthood of ancient Thebes (Luxor).

The calendar although once based on observations of the moon and sun throughout the cycle of the year, was later to become an arbitrary production, sanctified by authority and 'tradition'. Hence even when the dates on the civil calendar were blatantly out of phase with the actual seasons, everyone had to go along with it and indeed even the King was forbidden to interfere.

Some would argue that the Theban priesthood favoured this kind of obscurity. It provided them with yet another role as guardians of arcane knowledge needed to make the calendar coincide with actual events. It became their professional domain as it were.

Modern Egyptophiles may see nothing wrong with this occult role being appropriated by the priesthood. They like the fact that priest developed this hidden knowledge. For me personally I don't think that way. The obscuration of what had once been common knowledge seems to me a pretty hollow mystery.

Further, it might be one of those moments in human history when we became more alienated from our environment. Standing as we do at the end of an historical trend whereby we have insulated ourselves from nature, and are happy to blank out the drama of the night sky behind an all pervasive light polluting city street.

But it was not always so, even in ancient Egypt, there was once a simple calendar that every man and woman could understand and use. Coincidentally, this would also have been the calendar used by the citizens of ancient Ombos, the citadel of Seth that I described in such detail in *The Bull of Ombos*. When Herodotus visited Egypt CIRCA 450BCE, he noted that the oldest Ennead or Company of Heaven consisted of twelve gods - one for each month.[4] I would remind you again, that many of the very oldest pieces of Egyptian mythology concern the mysteries and cycles of the moon. Foremost amongst these, would be the myths of the Contending of Horus and Seth, which many an eminent scholar has concluded must be related to the waxing and waning of the moon.

So now, I want to explore a little further the working of that archaic lunar calendar especially the deities associated with the thirty days of the lunar month. In **Figure 17** you can see the northern constellations (Hippo, etc) flanked by two rows of deities. Parker[6] says that a late text by an astrologer called Petosiris (not to be confused with the Theban priest of same name) identifies these deities with the circumpolar stars in general. Parker *et al* have so far been unable to find any astronomical basis for this association.

> 'The deities usually have a lunar disk on their head, and on the body there are at times stars at such points as wrists, elbows, shoulders, navel, knees and ankles. These stars may be shown as circles as is also the practice with the decans and the constellations on occasion. In the orientation of the deities there is complete consistency. Isis, if present, and the deities which follow her *always* stand behind *Hippo,* whether

that figure be to the right or left side of the constellations. The other row of deities then takes the opposite side. The association of Isis with *Hippo* has been discussed above.' [7]

We must then acknowledge Richard Parker as the discoverer of the division of the lunar deities into two groups – one lining up behind Isis and Hippo and the other lining up 'against' them. The obvious assumption to me is to see these as representing the deities of the waxing and waning moon or the two halves of the lunar month.

The Senmut astrological ceiling does not exhibit a full complement of thirty deities, one for each of the lunar days. Some appear to be missing from the frieze. Could it be that those depicted are in some way special days? - I think so. But as a convenient key to the Senmut arrangement, we are going to use a later monument that graces the temple of Horus at Edfu. This temple was built at the behest of Ptolemy VIII (Euergetes 'Benefactor' II) sometime 145 - 116 BCE, and therefore more than a thousand years later than the Senmut

---

Figure 17: Senmut was queen Hatshepsut's (1503-1482BC) most favoured courtier, possibly lover. This detail shows all the important characteristics of this complex glyph: the central scene with the Northern constellations, Horus (An) harpooning the Bull (Mes), shown with red hoofs and Hippo (Tawaret) holding the flint mooring post surmounted by a red circle representing the celestial pole. The groups of gods to the right and left are the attendant deities, including another form of Seth (Imy-sha) and Isis. Parker says these attendants are deities of the lunar days, which have no obvious connection with the Northern constellations. The twelve circles, subdivided into twenty-four are also connected with lunar festivals.[5]

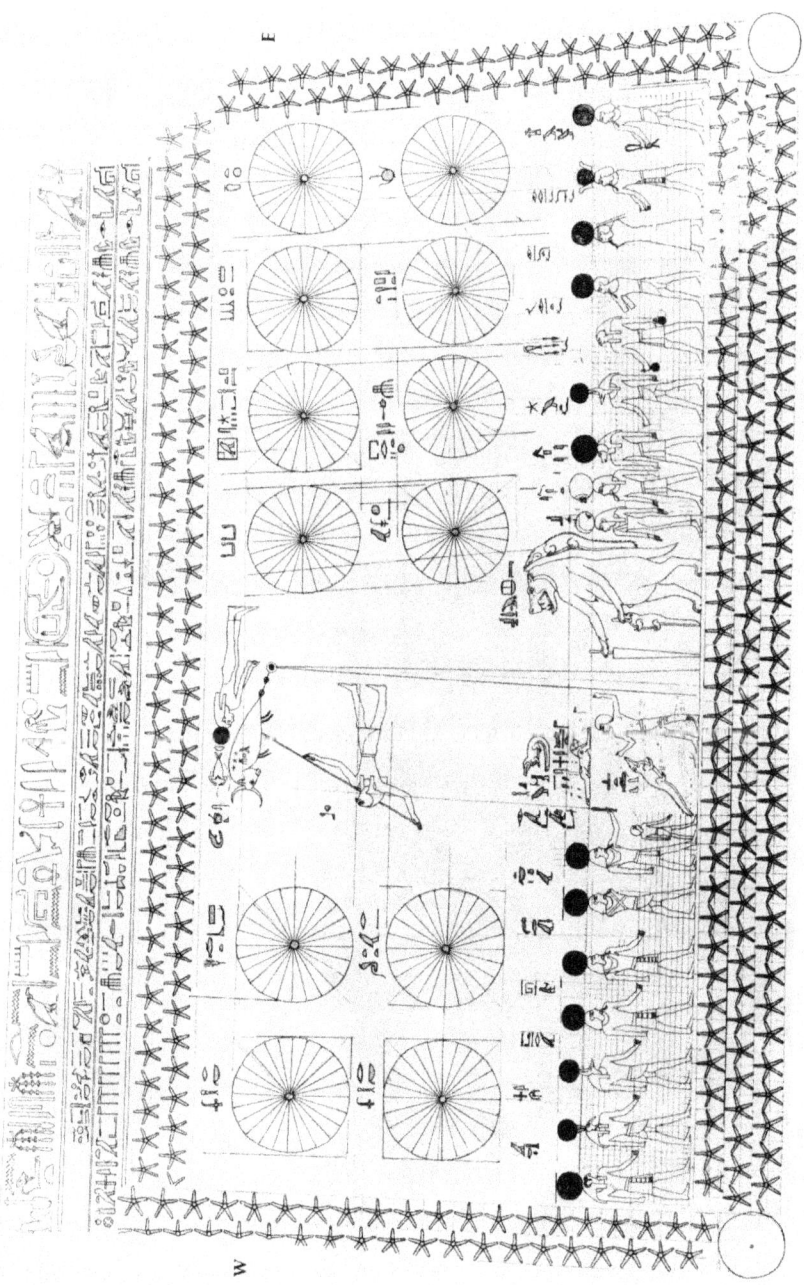

ceiling. It can be seen on the north wall of the outer hypostyle hall (**see Table 7**).[6]

The monument is 'Hellenistic' which has pejorative sense as contrasted with 'Hellenic'. Hellenistic is like 'Greekish' - a scornful term for the culture of the three centuries between Alexander and the 'complete envelopment of the area by the expanding might of Rome'.[7]

In fact, Hellenistic culture is rather dynamic and it is becoming rather untenable to dismiss it as some degenerate afterthought. Hellenistic texts are actually quite careful with their older sources, and often record some very ancient traditions indeed. See for example the myth of 'Atlantis' cited in my earlier book *Tankhem*.[8]

The Deities of the Waxing or 'Bright' half of the month

As you might expect, the division of the deities into bright and dark halves reflects Egyptian mythology. This is contained in the so-called Heliopolitan cosmology, headed up by Atum-Ra. In its later development it is combined with other systems by the Theban theologians, giving us the syncretic sun-god Amun-Ra or simply Ra.

Ra has two children – Shu & Tefnut (wind and moisture). When they die, they are succeeded nine 'days' later by a further divine couple, Geb and Nuit, (earth and space).

But these two, being more unruly than their parents, give birth to four offspring. This breaks the divine order, and thus the next generation of gods, who are closer to humans, are sometimes viewed as the accursed gods. These are Osiris, Isis, Seth and Nephthys.

Not surprisingly, this 'cursed' generation of gods, like any family, soon fall into dispute. To cut a long story short: Osiris is murdered by his 'evil' brother Seth. Seth then 'usurps' his kingdom, attempting to seduce Isis and disenfranchise his 'rightful' heir Horus. As a monomyth, this pattern enters into many later stories, for example it may well be the basis of Shakespeare's drama – Hamlet. Some of the intricacies of the myth are analyzed in more detail in my earlier book *The Bull of Ombos*, and I do not want to go over that now. Suffice it to say that the lunar gods of the bright fortnight would broadly speaking fall into the Osirian camp, whereas those of the dark fortnight are broadly Sethian or Typhonian in nature.

This Osirian 'spin' on history is already fully formed when the first mythological texts were composed and inscribed in pyramids of the 5th dynasty. So it's hardly surprising to find this reflected in the myths of the astrological ceiling of the Vizier Senmut. To read the older material that lies barely visible beneath the surface requires a measure of careful detective work.

The deities of the bright half line up to the right behind the Hippo goddess - and almost always begin with Isis. All the deities of the moon's bright half share associations with the god Horus. This reflects the thesis laid out in my previous books, that the Conflict

Table 7: Complete key to gods and festivals of the lunar month (dark half) - Ptolemaic		
Lunar day	Edfu second series	
	god or entity	feast name
1	Thoth	new moon feast
2	Horus, avenger of his father	new crescent day
3	Osiris	arrival day
4	Amseti	going forth of the sem priest (*prt šm*)
5	Hapi	offering on the altar (*iḫt ḥr ḫiwt*)
6	Tiamutef	sixth day (*šnt*)
7	Kebsenef	first quarter day (*dnit*)
8	Iretef	
	'two eyes of his father'	feast of first day of quarter (*tp*)
9	Iredjetef	
	'the god who engenders himself'	feast of fish (*kȝp*)
10		feast of the stain
11	man with club	festival of the light of the sun & of vengeance
12	Harhar - god holding unknown instrument	day of writing
13	Thoth	feast of effusion of the eyes
14	Amon Ra	Feast of revelation/sanctity of the ram
15	goddess	feast of shimmering moonlight

Table 7: Gods and Festivals of the Lunar Month (from Edfu)

Table 7: Complete key to gods and festivals of the lunar month (dark half) - Ptolemaic

Lunar day	Edfu second series	
	god or entity	feast name
16	second birth of the flower (*ms prhw*)	the day that fills his word (*mh.f ti.f*)
17	horus, with lotus scepter (*hry ti.f*)	of truth (*mᶜ3 hb*)
18	Ahi - brother of Hathor	of the moon
19	Seth, Bull of Ombos	listening to their words
20	Anubis	choice (*štp*)
21	Anubis	*ᶜprw*
22	the serpent Na (*nᶜ*)	strength of sothis (*ph ᶜspdt*)
23	grand serpent Na (*nᶜ wr*)	denit (*dnit*)
24	red serpent Na	occultation (*knhw*)
25	Shem (The stranger)	purification (*w3b*)
26	Iri-mery-ef (*iri-mry-f*)	of going forth (*prtw*)
27	Wenet, hare goddess	the answer
28	Khnoum	going forth in the sky
29	Horus, his father's offspring	night vigil
30	The god Nehes	rescue (?)

of Horus & Seth was originally connected with the mysteries of the waxing and waning moon. The conflict or dialectical relationship between Horus & Seth, is actually much older than the roles these gods take in the later mythology of Osiris.

The astrological ceiling of Senmut provides us with a good paradigm. It is probably significant that it shows just seven dieties in the bright half of the month - and this is broadly in line with other records of six main rites celebrated during the month (see chapter 2) i.e. New moon; First crescent; Going forth of Sem priests; Sixth day feast; Full moon.

1. Isis (*3st*) - 'The throne'

Isis is almost always present on monuments (*Supernatural Assault* for more background on this most famous of goddesses).[11]

2. Imsety (*imsti*)

Next come the Four Sons of Horus (born by Hathor?) shown here in the traditional order of the Pyramid Texts.[9] Imseti is a man-headed deity, shown in many images as bearing a traditional flint knife. As one of the spirits of the dead, Imseti is dedicated to the stomach, which was removed from the deceased during the mummification process, and stored in its own canopic jar.

3. Hapy (*hpy*)

The second son of Horus is baboon-headed.

4. Duamutef (*dw3mwt.f*)

The third son of Horus is consistently jackal-headed.

Lunar day	Bright or Horian half (lined up behind Hippo-)	lunar day	Dark of Sethian half (lined up behind Meshkeneh, Bull of Ombos, the Plough)
	deity		deity
1	Isis	16	(Ir-m-awA) who-acts-violently
2		17	
3		18	Tekenu (*tknw*)
4	Imsety	19	
5	Hapy	20	
6	Duamutef	21	
7	Kebehsenuf	22	Shed-Keru (*šd-hrw*) - the troublemaker
8		23	Nehes (*nhs*) - the watcher
9	Manitef	24	Aaner (*ꜥ-nr*) - great of fear
10	Irendjef	25	Seth (*Imy-sh-ntr*) - who is in the god's Booth
11	Irenrenefdjesef	26	
12	Hakow	27	
13		28	
14		29	Hor-Hekenew (*hr-hknw*) - Horus be praised
15		30	

Table 8: Lunar days from astronomical ceiling of Vizier Senmut. This hypothetical arrangement is informed by information from later monuments including the Ptolemaic temple of Horus at Edfu.

5. Kebehsenuf (*ḳbḥ-snw.f*)

The fourth son of Horus is falcon-headed on all but two monuments. In the Senmut family the disk is characteristically omitted from his head.

6. Ma-enitef (*m3nit.f*)- 'Who-looks-at-his-father'

An aspect of Horus. The figure is consistently human-headed but the arms vary greatly. A number of monuments have the arms raised with the hands before the face.

7. Iren-djedef (*Ir.n-dt.f*) - 'Whom-his-body-made'

Original name, 'Who-acts-with-his-body'. The figure of the deity is human-headed and mummiform. In the others he is human-headed and armless. In Senmut's main group he wears a long skirt.

8. Iren-renef-djesef (*ʿIr-rn.f-ds.f*) - 'Who-made-his-own-name'

Generally the arms are before the human-headed figure which has a plume on either side of the disk on the head, but the figure is sometimes armless.

9. Hakow (*h3kw*) - 'Plunderer'

The deity is human-headed and is characterized by the object he holds with both hands before his body. In Senmut's main group this object resembles a short looped rope, with the hands holding both ends below the loop. In other monuments the figure holds an ankh, sistrum, knife and sometimes the Was (*w3s*) scepter, whose connection to the god Seth is discussed in *The Bull of Ombos* and *Tankhem*.

This god seems out of place in the bright half, but maybe this again demonstrates how there is no impermeable barrier between bright and dark halves of the month; the seeds of the dark are present in the light and vice versa. It is tempting to see some connection with Heka (*ḥk3*) - magick - although the spelling is different.

The Moon's waning or dark half

The opposing row of deities always headed by Irem-awa vary in number. Senmut's main group has seven, the minimum number, but the other monuments list nine or ten, with the great majority having ten. Two alone have eleven.

1. Irem-awa (ʿIr-m-ʿw3) 'who-acts-violently'

The figure is human-headed and holds a club in one hand. With the exception of Nehes - none of these deities occur in the Ptolemaic lists and it is therefore difficult to assign particular lunar days to each. My arrangement is therefore speculative although based on some known parameters. For instance, the Seth like Irem-awa, probably has to stand opposite to Isis, as representing the first day of the dark half of the moon, just as she represents the new moon. Records from the Temple of Seth at Sepermeru, tell us of a goat sacrificed on the so-called 'day of rams', ie first day of the month's dark half.

Just after the full moon there is still a bit of a struggle between the 'darkness & light' - with the moon waning, but only on slightly reduced power. It is really the moon's final quarter where Seth and his companions really cluster. The days around the new moon are another matter entirely. Here, Horus and his followers begin the rally. For example:

> This was, then, a tradition widespread and of long standing, since it was incorporated in three temple calendars, all of varying dates of composition. Horus was born on the second day of the lunar month . . . Why was Horus born on the second lunar day? We have seen that on that day, the new crescent normally appeared. Moreover, the tutelary deity of the second lunar day is Hor-nedjitef (*ḥr nḏ it..f*) - 'Horus, avenger of his father.' That suggests some connection with Osiris. . . The dead Osiris as the vanished moon. His day of embalmment is the day when the moon is never visible. But on the following day, he shines forth from his temple at sunset, just as the crescent moon normally appears on the second day of the lunar month at sunset. If this be the resurrection of Osiris, which it certainly seems to be, since he wakes from his sleep and takes his place in the sky, then it is small wonder that Horus, son of Osiris, is born on the same lunar day on which his father is reborn.'[10]

2. Tekenu (*tknw*) - 'the cup'

Armless human headed figure. The name means 'cup' - and is also the original name for the first month of the year, and is a reference to a feast of drunkenness or perhaps intoxication, used in one of those special Blue Lily cups described in *Supernatural Assault*. Tekenu also plays some mysterious role in the Ceremony of Opening the Mouth.

3. Shed-Keru (*šd-ḥrw*) - 'The troublemaker'
Human headed figure with bent arms.

4. Nehes (*nhs*) - 'The watcher'
Human, sometimes falcon headed figure.

5. Aaner (*ʿ3-nr*) - 'great of fear'
Human although often also jackal headed figure.

6. Seth (*Imy-sḥ-nṯr*) - 'Who is in the god's booth'
Seth headed figure although some later monuments substitute an ibis or jackal.

7. Hor-hekenew (*ḥr-ḥknw*) - 'Horus be praised'
Falcon headed figure.

Additional days found in other monuments.

8. Aa-pehetey (*ʿ3-pḥty*) - 'Great of strength'
Usually human headed sometimes animal headed with two knives.

9. Akes (*ʿks*)
Human headed deity usually paired with Hepui (see next). The name apparently denotes some part of the royal apparel, and is later written *Hekes*.

10. Hepui (*ḥpwy*)
Hepui is human-headed and no doubt a personification of the two royal sunshades. He is usually paired with Akes.

11. Duamutef (*dw3-mwt.f*)
Falcon-headed deity, found in this position on just two monuments.

12. King or Other
As in the opposite row just two monuments close the row with the figure of the king. Petosiris adds a mummiform figure with the legend *s3.f* - 'his son'. Only one monument has two figures after Hepui.

Conclusion: how to use this information
Records show that although every lunar day had an association with a particular deity - only about seven days in the first half of the month were the focus of any consistent religious activity. These basic seven days might well have varied within specific sects, and in fact I suggest that the "Companions of Seth" would have their focus on the dark third week of the lunar month, although other records show day sixteen was also important to the Sethians - see next chapter.

Notes
1. Richard A (1950 : 50) *The Calendars of Ancient Egypt*, Chicago
2. Edwards, I E S (1950) *Oracular Amuletic Decrees of the Late New Kingdom*, 2 vols, Hieratic Papyris in the British Museum 4th series. L3. My paraphrase, the original inumerates every month individually. The Book of 'That which is in the Year' - Egyptian title *Imy ḥry rnp.t*
3. Morgan, Mogg (2006 : 104-5) *The Bull of Ombos: Seth & Egyptian Magick II*, Mandrake.
4. Herodotus II.4
5. Parker (1950); Neugebauer O & Parker, R (1962) *Ancient Egyptian Astronomical Texts*, 4 vols, Brown University.

6   Parker (1950 : 3)

7   Neugebauer O & Parker, R (1962). Parker further observes that there are many variations in the way the names of the lunar deities are written just as there are in other details, such as the list of decans or names of the constellations. These variations fall into various groups, for instance some being more common to particular dynasties etc.

8. Neugebauer & Parker (1962) Plate 30A

9. Lewis, Nephtali (1986: 1) *Greeks in Ptolemaic Egypt*, Oxford.

10. Morgan, Mogg (2005 : 155) *Tankhem: Seth & Egyptian Magick*, Mandrake

11. PT 1092, 1333, 1339, 1548, 2078. With some exceptions, Isis appears with the name of 'Imseti' above her figure, while that god himself is absent.

12. Parker (1950 : 60-61)

13. Chassinat, E (1918, 1928) *Temple d'Edfou*, MMAF 21-31

Another mysterious thing about Chassinat's wonderful documentation of the monument is room M on the eastern side -called 'hadit' (*bhdt*) or the 'hall of the magician' - presumably a local tradition as the room itself concerns the mysteries of the lion headed goddess Mehet (*mḥt*) aggressive consort of Onuris, and the Ennead who watch over Osiris.

Figure 18: Astrological frieze from Temple of Horus at Edfu.
The following drawings are from the astrological frieze in the Hellenistic Temple of Horus of Edfu. The frieze is situated on the northern wall, below the architrave of the outer hypostyle hall. The standard publication of the temple is E Chassinat, these images are from H Brugsch (1857) *Monumens de l'Égypt*, Berlin.

The frieze shows a complete set of fourteen deities, plus Thoth for the fifteenth or full moon day. This sequence differs from and is not seen in any monument before the Ptolemaic period, and may well be a Greek innovation, although inspired by Egyptian forms. This sequence omits the dark or 'Sethian' half of the month, which is what one might expect in a temple dedicated to Horus.[11]

The sequence begins on the top left, with the last of 36 decans, the final one a recumbant deity in a boat, representing a planet or constellation. The procession of lunar days begins with the god Tum, whose foot can be seen foot resting on the first of a fourteen step staircase:

Day 1 Tum
Day 2 Shu
Day 3 Tefnut
Day 4 Seth (?)
Day 5 Geb
Day 6 Nuit
Day 7 Horus

Day 8 Isis
Day 9 Nephthys
Day 10 Horus
   in 'the Big House'
Day 11 Amseti
   'Four Sons of Horus'
Day 12 Hapy
Day 13 Duamutef
Day 14 Kebehsenuf

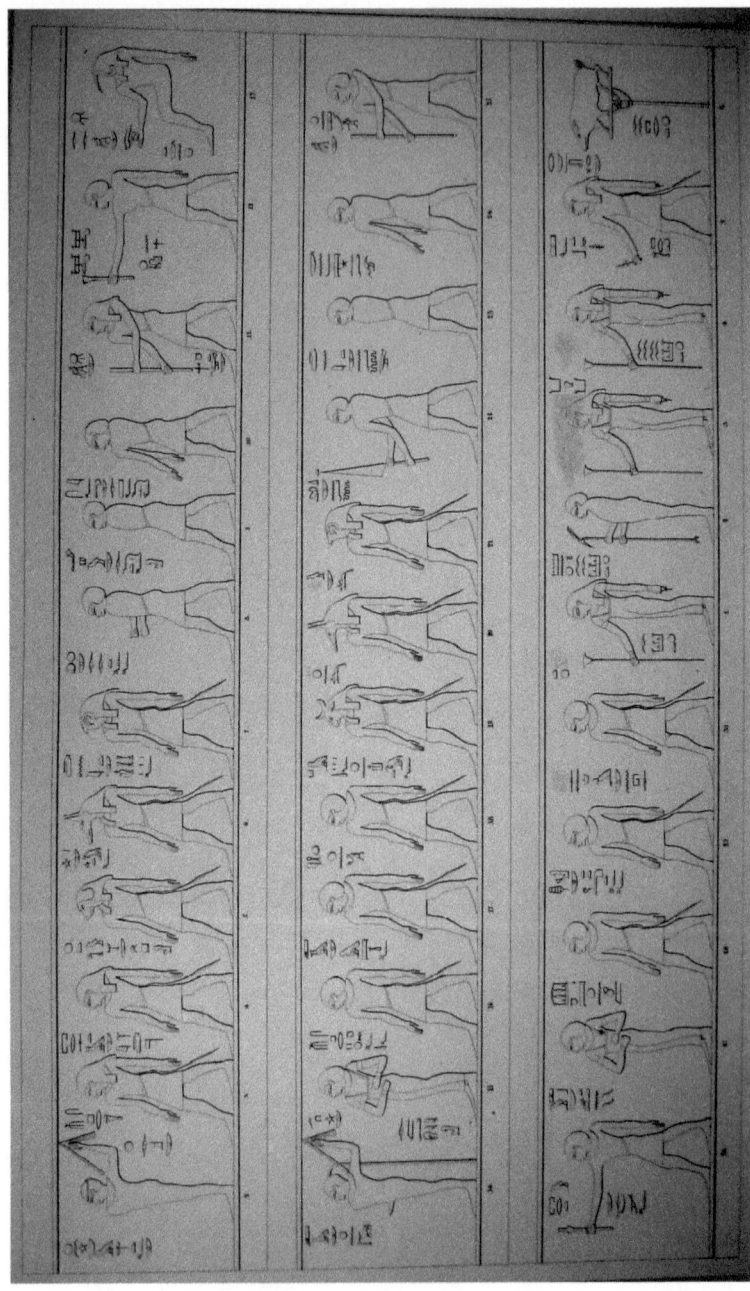

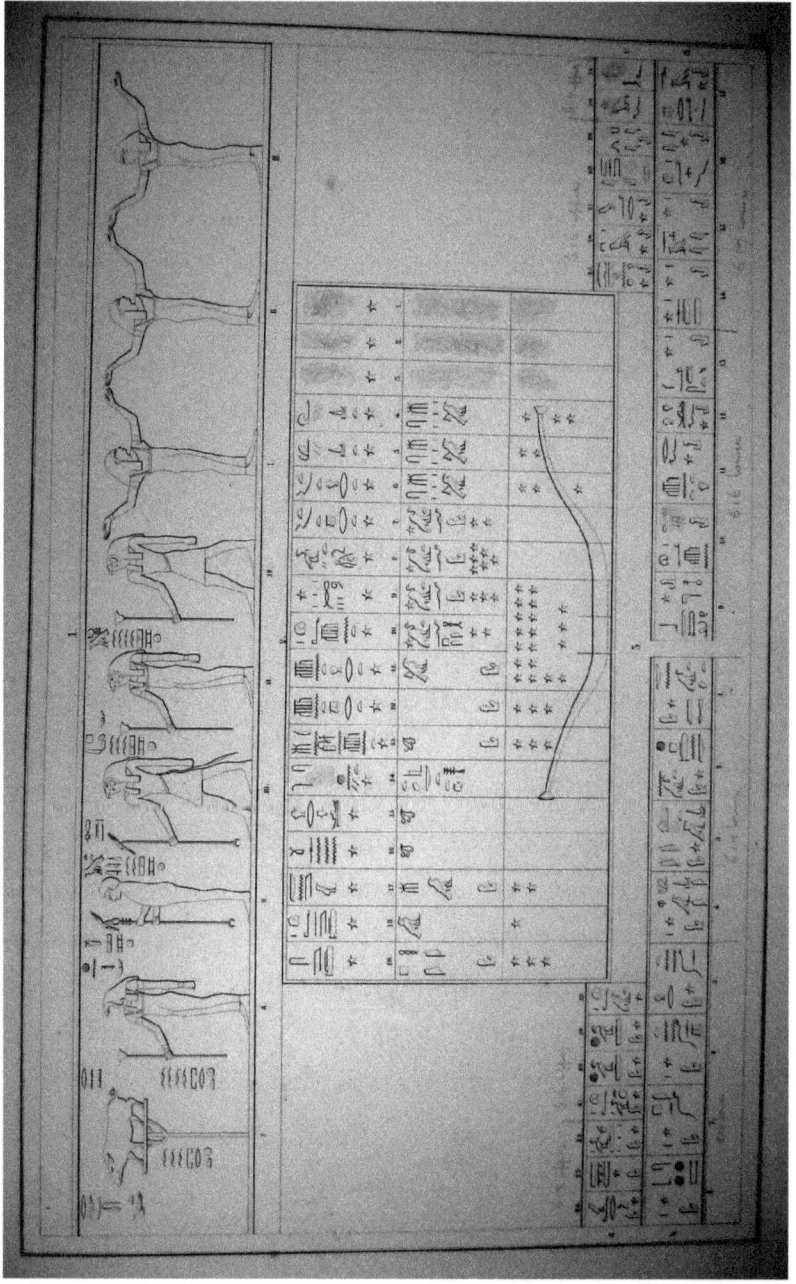

5 Oracles & Lunar Omina

'I pass to other inventions of the Egyptians. They assign each month and each day to some god; they can tell what fortune and what end and what disposition a man shall have according to the day of his birth. This has given material to Greeks who deal in poetry. They have made themselves more omens than all other nations together; when an ominous thing happens they take note of the outcome and write it down; and if something of a like kind happens again they think it will have a like result.'

Herodotus, II 82

(Translation by A D Godley, Loeb Classical Library.)

Egyptian lunar omens are found in one rare Egyptian text. Its rarity was enough to convince scholars such as Richard Parker[1] that it must have been copied from a Babylonian original. But other more recent studies have reinstated the text as part of an independent Egyptian tradition of lunar observation.[2] This same tradition was still vibrant by the time of the Greek Magical Papyri which preserves several examples of lunar divination. For example:

'... Equip your eyes with green ... and black eyepaint. You should stand on a high place on the top of your house. You should speak to the moon when it fills the sound eye on the 15th day (ie: full moon), you being pure for three days. You should recite this spell . . . seven or nine times until he appears to you and speaks:

"Hail, SAKS AMOUN SAKS ABRASAKS for you are the moon, the great one of the stars, he who formed them. Listen to these things which I have said! Walk in accordance with the words of my mouth!

Reveal yourself to me, THAN / THANA THANATHA . . . this is my correct name". [3]

Egyptian lunar omina were always observed on the 15th day i.e. full moon day (*semedet*). One possible exception to this was in Dakhleh where oracles were made on the basis of observations on the sixteenth day. The sun and moon can appear in the sky together on the sixteenth day and this is no doubt part of its significance.

[The Dakhleh Stele mentions a feast of Seth celebrated on the 25th day of the fourth month of winter which may originally have been a new moon feast. An astronomical ceiling also from Dakhleh has a deity of the eighth lunar month which, although missing was probably meant to represent Seth (see footnote 4).]

The Dakhleh Oasis was a focus for the worship of Seth right until to the very end of Egyptian history. I described in chapter 3 the discovery of an astrological ceiling from a tomb at Deir el Haggar in the Dakhleh Oasis, and what it reveals about the worship of Seth in the desert regions.[4] The Ashmolean Museum in Oxford possesses two interesting stele from Dakhleh - the larger of which reveals many more interesting details about the cult, including an

Figure 19: Oracular Judgement Stele, the larger of two stele retrieved from the Dakhleh Oasis and now in the Ashmolean Museum, Oxford. 325 x 243mm. This and the other example photographed by William Spiegelberg (see fn4).

oracle from his temple used to settle a tricky local dispute over water management. The illustration shows this stele together with a sketch that reveals the finer details. This stele is from the 21st dynasty (1075-715BCE). It shows an obscure fetish together with the possible sanctuary of Seth being adored by twin Hathors.

Gardiner is unsure what to make of this but to me it is further indication of the thesis I suggested in *The Bull of Ombos*, that the goddess Hathor may have been the original consort of the god Seth and in some far flung Egyptian places, this tradition was maintained. Interestingly the fetish shown in the Dakhleh Stele resembles that found at Abydos and is presumed to be the severed head of Osiris. There a many other examples of Egyptian worship of the severed head, including that of Hathor, Osiris, Bes to name but a few. This practice is very old and has particular cultic resonance to the Sethians.

THE RITUAL YEAR IN ANCIENT EGYPT

Figure 20: Second and smaller of the Dakhleh Stele, sandstone, this one records a gift of offerings to Horus at a local temple.

For this and other reasons discussed elsewhere, I think it safe to assume that Seth could well have been associated with full moon omina and Horus with those connected with the new moon.

The text of lunar omens that forms the basis for this chapter was amongst several related texts first published by Richard Parker. The papyrus contains two texts written after the Persian takeover and therefore according to Parker, Babylonian in derivation although given a reworking by the Egyptian astronomers.

However, Babylonian oracles were distinctive in that they seem to have been made on the basis of the crescent moon. The voluminous *Enuma Anu Enlil* has so far only revealed omens for the crescent moon although, most scholars think when the whole of the *Enuma* is translated it will reveal full moon omens.[5]

The first text studied by Parker presents omens connected with the lunar eclipse. Depending on time of year, these omens are allocated to the surrounding countries in a manner similar to that used by the Babylonians. The Egyptians merely re-edited the text substituting countries that were to them more relevant. Which also serves to show the inclusive nature of ancient paganism.

The second text concerns observations of the moon on certain days, taking note of various phenomena such as halos, patterns, shadows, colours etc., and these are then interpreted. Each interpretation is accompanied by a drawing or vignette of the moon. This kind of observation is unknown otherwise than this text, but it does fit the development of Egyptian oracles from Ramesside and other periods.[6]

Example: Col XVI
If you see the disk divided at one place, death at one place, death shall occur at the beginning of the year.
(The vignette shows the moon with this division.)

Egyptian Oracles

Egyptian oracles went through a long and complex development over thousands of years. By the post pharaonic times, incubation shrines were still appearing. For example, the Kushite god Mandulis had a shrine at Talmis on 3rd cataract that attracted the attentions of the intellectual pagans of the times. These young men and women of the Greco-Roman world, gave these gods a new content they probably never previously possessed. These shrines became objects of pilgrimage and centres of many extant inscriptions.[7]

Using red ochre, these pilgrims left so-called 'proskynema' or votive graphiti. They have a gnostic quality where the actual historicity of the shrine is less important than the magical quest itself:

'Then I knew Mandulis to be the sun,
all powerful Eternity (Aion)'

The Osireion at Abydos became the focus of another celebrated oracle shrine - first to Serapis then Bes.[8] Bes was probably a priestly innovation of the existing popular oracle. The secret crypt in the mortuary temple might well be for the purpose of voice oracles. This shrine was eventually suppressed by emissaries of

Constantine II in 359AD. The oracle archive was then used to persecute previous supplicants.

The tradition develops a more literary form – which in turn mutates to things like the 'knuckle bone oracle' (*sortes*) of Greek Magicaa Papyri fame – which provides written questions and answers.[9] The diviner is known as a *mantis*. Sosipatra and her son Antoninus were famous manti, whose prognostications forced the downfall of the Alexandrian temple

The later Christian prophets stayed away from these sanctuaries. They remained on the periphery, which in the end gave them a wider, more transregional authority. Their most famous exercise in repackaging was the Oracle of the Potter.[10]

The prophesies of the potter allude to the intellectual resistance to Greek control in 130BCE, and the hope of an apocalypse and new order. The Greeks were here equated with Seth as the enemy of the Horus kingship they wanted to restore. The roots of apocalypse lie in chaos to be followed by new order. There were to be nine days of chaos before this new order established itself, just as there were said to be nine days between the death of Shu and ascension of Geb. The Lamb and Potter oracles were sacred to potter god Khnum. They made use of symbolic numbers such as nine, as in the nine members of the ancient Egyptian ennead or 'company of heaven'. This nine also lends itself to 9, 90, 900 codes. All of this finds its way into the apocalyptic oracle or 'Book of Revelation' that rounds off the Christian *New Testament*.

Moon sight meditation:

I am now close to the end of what I hope is another useful piece of the enigma that is Typhonian magick. It merely remains for me to set out the surviving part of the text on lunar omina. Given that there are some gaps, this lends itself to a bit of investigation by the contemporary practitioner. I sometimes go out on the full moon day, the day after or one of the "white nights" and observe the moon, perhaps using a technique such as 'moon sight' meditation. This stems from a Japanese Zen technique. Look at the moon, then close your eyes for a moment. Open them again, and then close. Continue until you have a good afterimage of the moon in your mind's eye. Or draw down the moon so that its vibrancy flows through you. When you come to write up your experiences note down how the moon looks, especially if there are any strange after images, clouds, arorae etc. Welcome to the project of reassembling the lost knowledge of the ancient Egyptians.

Notes:

1. Parker, Richard A (1959) *Vienna Demotic Papyri on Luna Omina*, Brown University, USA.

2. Vernus, P (1981) 'Omina Calendériques et Comptabilité d'offrandes sur une tablette Hiératique de la XVIIIe Dynastie - Papyrus Leyden I 346.' RDE 33 pp.89-124.

3. PDM xiv 695-700, Betz, HD (1986) *Greek Magical Papyri in Translation*, p 232.

4. The Dakhleh Stele (Ashmolean 1893/107) Published in Gardiner (1933) JEA 19 pp19-30 pls 5-7) Photographs in Spiegelberg, W (1899) vols XIX (1989) & XXV (1903). *Recueil de Travaux relatifs à la Philologie*. [Kaper (1995) 'The Astronomical Ceiling of Deir el Haggar in the Dakhleh Oasis' *JEA* 81 pp.151-73. For the 'Dakhleh Stele' see also Gardiner, A H (1933) *JEA* pp. 19-33. For information on Seth worship in Dakhleh see Osing (1985) *MDAIK* 41, 229-33.]

5. Reiner, Erica (1975 to date), with David Pingree, *Babylonian Planetary Omens*, (The Enuma Anu Enlil) Brill/Styx.

6. Parker, Richard (1962) *A Saite Oracle Papyrus from Thebes*. Interesting in a different way as it records a consultation of the oracle at Luxor on whether a priest should take on another priestly job with Khonsu. Has an important essay by Cerny in which he discusses the mechanics of the oracle – proposing that when the priests carry the barque forward that could be affirmative, whereas walking away is negative.

7. Frankfurter, David (1994 : 166) 'The Magic of writing and the writing of magic. The power of the word in Egyptian and Greek tradition.' *Helios* 21 (1924) pp.189 - 221, 199-205; Sayce 1894 for inscriptions; Nock

8. Frankfurter (1994 : 170)

9. Frankfurter (1994)

10. Koerien L (1970) 'The Potter Oracle', *Proceedings of the XIIth International Congress of Papyrology*.

Appendix:
Egyptian Lunar observations

Several sections of this rare Egyptian manuscript are missing and some of the vignettes are out of position in the original but have been moved to their correct column where possible. I suggest the reader makes good the gaps with some your own observations

Key

DY = DARK YELLOW

B = BLACK

R = RED

LB = LIGHT BLUE

G = GREY

DG = DARK GREY

Col VIII	Col VII
If you see a disk coloured completely on the 15th day (semedet) - there being a black disk around it - great fighting will happen.	If you see the disk rising southwards there being one star outside it you are to say: great poverty shall occur in the entire land. death and the king shall slay his adversaries. barley and emmer shall be abundant. But the entire land in conflict and people eat snakes in their houses.
another: one disk inside it: death throught the entire land but the harvest plentiful.	if you see the moon at any time when . . . the chief of egypt shall send to the chiefs of the foreigners.
	DY B

Col X	Col IX
	DY ⬤
If you see the moon coloured with one star within: Death shall occur	lif you see the moon coloured completely and with red rays shining downward: great fighting against the king but harvest good.
Nothing preserved	If you see the moon, its northern part black, its southern illumined: King shall approach king and chiefs of foreigners shall slay their enemies.

	Col XI
● ◉ ●	LB ⬤
	missing
◎	✻ ◯ ✻

Col XIII	Col XII
○	✶ ✶ ✶
if you see the moon's disk rising and lighting up the sails of the day a great inundation. barley and emmer abundant death for all creatures within three years.	if you see the moon's disk coloured with three stars in a row. great trouble for the king who prevails over his enemies in all directions.
another: moon coloured downward in red. egypt shall mourn a great wind in the sky harvest plentiful. strength.	another: if you see the moon's disk coloured with a black star inside: fighting and trouble men shall eat his neighbours things.
R ◐	✶

Col XV	Col XIV
Missing	If you see the moon's disk rising in the east on new year's day ($h3t\ rnpt$). the southern area covered:death at the beginning of the year.
Another: Moon entirely black apart from a red disk inside: revolt in the army which rules like a woman with her children.	Another: If you see the moon's disk illumined there being a star inside it:confusion reigns for three years.ploughing but no harvest.
	G DG

Col XVII	Col XVI
◐	
missing	If you see the moon's disk divided in one place. death at the beginning of the year (ḥȝt rnpt)
missing	Another: If you see the moon's disk two colours in a hole: King shall approach king. armies fighting children shall (?) older children.

Col XIX	Col XVIII
	⬤
red (rest missing)	If you see the moon's disk entirely one colour: the northland shall (?) good things harvest plentiful barley & emmer king lives a long time death of a star good inundation
missing	missing

Col XXI	Col XX

Col XXIII	Col XXII

Col XXV	Col XXIV

Col XXVII	Col XXVI

Col XXIX	Col XXVIII

Appendix 1
Lunar Diary

'I draw down the bright blue moon from the sky
though brazen cymbals crash and thunder
to keep her in her place
even the chariot of the sun, my grandfather,
grows pale at my song
and I drain the colour from the dawn for my potions'
Ovid Metamorphoses

In my book *Tankhem* I included a lunar calendar based on the twenty-eight mansions of the moon. Since then I have revised my opinion on lunar observations moving closer to the original Egyptian model of the thirty days of the lunar month. So whilst the schema put forth in Tankhem is still valid I now recommend the following blank diary for recording of various observations.

There is a great deal of magical work that can be coordinated with such a diary. *Followers of Horus* will find it advantageous to synchronise their work with the period around the new moon. On the other hand, the *Companions of Seth* will find work advantageous during the 'white nights' of the full moon, especially the fifteenth and sixteenth days, whose significance is fully attested by the ancient Egyptian sources discussed in this volume. For further guidance, the adept is recommended to approach to the Ombos 'House of Life.'

The Ancient Egypt's Archaic Lunar Calendar				Sheet No ......
Solar Day	Egyptian	Translation	Phase	Notes
	pesedeteyw	new moon	1	
	tep 3bed	new crescent day	2	
	meseper	arrival day	3	
	prt sem	going forth of the cem priest	4	
	3het h3t	offerings on the altar	5	
	senet	sixth day	6	
	den3t	part day, first quarter day	7	
	tep		8	
	k3p		9	
	sif		10	
	setet		11	
reading uncertain	[hieroglyphs]		12	
	m33 sty		13	
	si3w		14	
	semedet	half-moon day, full moon	15	

*vocalic 'e' added for ease of reading

The Ancient Egypt's Archaic Lunar Calendar					Sheet No ......
Solar Day	Egyptian	Translation	Phase	Notes
	mešeper šen-new	second arrival day	16	
	šȝw		17	
	iʿh	day of the moon	18	
	šedem medew.ef		19	
	šetep		20	
	ʿperew		21	
	ph ʿsepedet		22	
	denit	part day, last quarter day	23	
	kenehw		24	
	šetet		25	
	peret		26	
	wŠb		27	
	heb-šed newet	the going forth of Nuit	28	
	ʿhȝ		29	
	peret Min	the going forth of Min	30	

Bibliography

Abbreviations:

BAR: Beasted, James Henry (1906-7) Ancient records of Egypt: historical documents from the earliest times to the Persian conquest / collected, edited and translated with commentary

EES: Egyptian Exploration Society

JARCE: Journal of the American Research Center in Egypt.

JEA: Journal of Egyptian Archaeology

JEOL: Jaarbericht van het Vooraziatrich Egyptisch Genootschap (Gezelschap) "Ex Orient Lux"

JJP: Journal of Juristic Papyrology

Lexikon: Lexikon de Ägyptologie (six vols) ed. Wolfgang Helck, Eberhard Otto, and Wolfhart Westendorf (Wiesbaden: O. Harrassowitz, 1972).

OMRU: Oudheidkundige Mededelingen Uit Het Rijks Museum ca Oudheden re Leiden.

RDeE: Revue d'Égyptology, Le Caire.

SAK = Studien zur Altägyptischa Kulture

Urk: Urkenden des ägyptischen Altertums; see Steindorff, G (1903)

Books

Allen, James P (1994) 'Reading a Pyramid' in *Homages à Jean Leclant*, Vol I pp. 5-28. Inst Français d'Archéologie Orientale.

Allen, James P (2005) 'The Art of Medicine in Ancient Egypt: an exhibition at the Metropolitan Museum of Art' *KMT* Vol 16 No 3 Fall edition, pp 43-47

Andrews, Carol AR (1995) 'An unusual source for magical texts' in *Studies in Ancient Egypt in honour of H S Smith*, EES pp.11-16.

Assmann, Jan (2001) *The Search for God in Ancient Egypt*, translated by David Lorton, Cornell.

Bác, Tamás A (1987) 'Prolegomena to the study of Calendars of Lucky and Unlucky days.' in Roccati A,.& A Siliotti *La Magia in Egitto ai Temple dei Faraoni.*

Baines, J (1990) 'Residual Knowledge, Hierarchy and Decorum' *JARCE* 27, pp1.22. Good overview of the issue of initiation

Baines, J & Malek, J, (2000) *Cultural Atlas of Ancient Egypt*, Andromeda

Bakir, A M, (1966) *The Cairo Calendar*, Cairo

Betz, H D (ed) (1986) *The Greek Magical Papyri in Translation*, Chicago.

Billigmeier, Jon-Christian (!987) 'Alphabets', entry in *Encyclopedia of Religions*, edited by Mircea Eliade, New York.

Bika Reed, (1987) *Rebel in the Soul*: translation of Berlin Papyrus 3023, Vermont.

Blackman, A. M. and H W Fairman (1943) 'The Myth of Horus at Edfu II', *JEA* 29.

Borchardt, L (1935) *Die Mittel zur zeitlichen Festiegung von Punkten der ägyptische Geshichte und ihre anwerdung.*

Borghouts, J (1987) 'Akhu and Hekau' in *La Magia in Egitto ai Temple dei Faraoni*, ed Roccati A & A Siliotti

Boylan, P (1922) *Thoth, the Hermes of Egypt*, OUP.

Breasted, James H (1906) *Ancient Records of Egypt*, 5 vols, Chicago.

Brewer, Douglas & Friedman, R F (1989) *Fish and Fishing in Ancient Egypt*, Aris & Phillips, UK.

Brugsch, Heinrich (1883) *Thesaurus Inscriptionum Aegyptiacarum*, 6 vols Leipzig.

Brugsch Heinrich (1891) *Die Aegyptolgie*, Leipzig.

Budge, E A Wallis (1901) *The Book of the Dead*, Kegan Paul.

Budge, E A Wallis (1906) *Egyptian Heaven & Hell*, Vol II, 'Book of Gates'.

Budge, E A Wallis (1923) *Hieratic Papyri in the British Museum*, 1st series. Contents: Festival Songs of Isis and Nephthys; Litanies of Sokar; Book of Overcoming Apep, Harris Magical Papyrus, Calendar of Lucky & Unlucky days.

Budge, E A Wallis (1923) *Hieratic Papyri in the British Museum*, 2nd series including Papyrus Sallier, British Museum

Cerny, J (1943) 'The meaning of Tyby', *Annales du Science des Antiquities* 43, pp173-181

Cheke, Aaron (2004)'Magic through the linguistic lenses of Greek mágos, Indo-European *mag(h)-, Sanskrit màyà and Pharaonic Egyptian ¡eká' in *Journal for the Academic Study of Magic II*, Mandrake of Oxford.

Collier Mark & B Manley (1998) *How to Read Egyptian Hieroglyphs*, BM London.

Clarke, John R (2003) *Roman Sex*, New York, Abrams.

Clagett, M (1995) *Ancient Egyptian Science II, Calendars, Clocks and Astronomy*, American Philosophical Society.

Daniel, Robert W. and Franco Maltomini (1990) Supplementum Magicum [in Zusammenarbeit mit der Arbeitsstelle fur Papyrusforschung im Institut fur Altertumskunde der Universitat Koln]

Darby, William (1977), Paul Ghalounqui & Louis Grivetti, *Food - The Gift of Osiris*, 2 vols London.

David, Antony E & Rosalie (1992) *A Biographical Dictionary of Ancient Egypt*, London.

Demarée, Robert J. (1983) *The 3ḫ ikr n Ra Stelae. On Ancestor Worship in Ancient Egypt*, Leiden.

Depuydt, L (1998) 'Hieroglyphic representation of the moon's absence' *(psḏntyw)* in *Festschrift W A Ward*.

Depuydt, L (1997) *Civil Calendar and Lunar Calendar in Ancient Egypt*, Leuven.

Depuydt, L (1999) *Fundamentals of Egyptian Grammar*, Frog Publishing, Massachusetts.

Derchain, Philippe (1962) *La Lune: mythes and rites*, Sources Orientales, Edition de Seuil, Paris.

Dieleman, Jacco (2005) *Priests, Tongues and Rites - the London-Leiden Magical Manuscripts and Translation in Egyptian Ritual* (100-300CE), Brill.

Doblhofer, E (1961) *Voices in Stone: The Decipherment of Ancient Scripts and Writing*, Souvenir.

Dornseiff, Franz (1925) *Das Alphabet in Mystik und Magie*, Berlin

Draco, Melusine (2001) *The Egyptian Book of Days - Calendars of Ancient Egypt*, Ignatus.

Draco, Melusine (2003) *The Egyptian Book of Nights* (zodiacs)

Duell, Prentice (1938) *The Mastaba of Mereruka*, 2 Vols, Chicago.

Edmonds, Radcliffe G III (??) 'At the Seizure of the Moon: the absence of the moon in the Mithras Liturgy' in *Prayer, Magick, and the Stars in the Ancient and Late Antique World*, Edited by Noegel, Walker & Wheeler, Pennsylvania State University Press.

Edwards, I E S (1950) *Oracular Amuletic Decrees of the Late New Kingdom*, 2 vols, Hieratic Papyris in the British Museum 4th series.

Emboden, William (1989) 'The Sacred Journey in Dynastic Egypt: Shamanistic Trance in the Context of the Narcotic Water Lily and the Mandrake, *Journal of Psychoactive Drugs* Vol 21(I) Jan-Mar pp 61-75.

Evans, L (2001) *Kingdom of the Ark*, Simon & Schuster.

Faulkner, (1956) *JEA* 42, text of *Berlin Pap 3024*.

Forbes, D C (2005) 'Set, Lord of Chaos' *KMT*, Vol 15 No 4 pp 67-71

Frankfurter, David (1998) *Religion in Roman Egypt*,

Frankfurter, David (1994) 'The Magic of writing and the writing of magic. The power of the word in Egyptian and Greek tradition.' *Helios* 21 (1924) pp.189 - 221, 199-205.

Fries, J (1992) *Visual Magick: A Handbook of Freestyle Shamanism*, Mandrake of Oxford.

Fries, J (2004) *Cauldron of the Gods: A Manual of Celtic Magick*, Mandrake of Oxford.

Fries, J (2005) *Helrunar: a Manual of Rune Magick*, Mandrake of Oxford.

Gardiner A H (1917) 'Professional Magicians in Egypt', *Proceedings of the Society for Biblical Archaeology 19*.

Gardiner, A H & K Sethe (1928) *Egyptian Letters to the Dead - mainly from the Middle Kingdom, copied, translated and edited*, EES.

Gardiner, A H (1931) *Chester Beatty Papyrus I*, Oxford University Press.

Gardiner A H (1938) 'The House of Life', JEA 24, 157-79pp.

Gardiner, A H (1941-48) *The Wilbour Papyrus*, 3 Vols, Oxford.

Gardiner, A H (1944) 'Horus the Behdetite' *JEA* 30 pp24ff.

Gardiner, A H (1947) *Ancient Egyptian Onomastica*, OUP.

Gardiner, AH (1950) 'The Baptism of Pharoah' *JEA* 36 pp3-12.

Gardiner A H (1955) *The Ramesseum Papyri*, OUP.

Gardiner, A H (1957) *Egyptian Grammar: being an introduction to the study of Hieroglyphs*, 3rd revised edition, Oxford.

Gasse, A (2004) 'Une Stèle d'horus sur les crocodiles à propos du <text C>' *Revue D'Égyptologie*, tome 55, pp23-44.

Gaster, Theodor H (1961) *Thespis: ritual, myth and drama in the ancient Near East*, New York.

Gautier J E & Jéquier, G (1902) *Fouilles de Licht*, L'Institute Français D'Archeologie Oriental, Vol 6.

Ginzel K F (1906) *Handbuch de Mathematischen und technischen chronologie*, Leipzig

Griffiths, J G (1960) *The Conflict of Horus and Seth*, Liverpool.

Gupta, S, Hoens, D K & Goudriaan T (1979) *Hindu Tantrism*, Leiden.

Harer W Benson (1985) 'Pharmacological and Biological Properties of the Egyptian Lotus' Hayes, JARCE XXII pp49-54

Herodotus, Translation by A D Godley, Loeb Classical Library

Hikade, Thomas (2003) 'Getting the ritual right - fishtale knives in predynastic Egypt' pp 137-152 in *Egypt - Temple of the Whole World - Studies in Honour of Jan Assmann*, Brill.

Hutton, R (1999) *The Triumph of the Moon: a history of modern pagan witchcraft*, OUP.

Kaper, O (1995 'The astronomical ceiling of Deir el Haggar in the Dakhla Oasis' JEA 81 151-73.

Katzeff, Paul (1990) *Moon Madness and other effects of the Full Moon*, Hale.

Kees, Herman (1923-4) *Horus and Seth als Götterpaar*, Göttingen

Kees, Hermann (1977) *Ancient Egypt*, Chicago UP.

Koefoed-Petersen, O, (1948) *Les Stèles Égyptiennes*, Copenhagen.

Kloetzli, R W (1985) 'Maps of Time - Mythologies of Descent: Scientific Instruments and the purāṇic Cosmograph' *History of Religions* 25 pp. 120-45.

Lajtar, A (1991) 'Proskynema - inscriptions of a corporation of Iron workers from Hermonthis in the temple of Hatshepsut in Deir el-Bahari; new evidence of Pagan cults in the 4th century ad', *Journal of Juristic Papyrology* 21 (1991) 53-70

Legge, F (1905) 'Magic Ivories of the Middle Kingdom' Proceedings of the Society of Biblical Archaeology, pp 130-152 + plates.

Leibovitch, J, (1943-45) 'Le griffon' parts I, II & III, *Bulletin de l'Institut d'Égypte, Le Caire.*, Nos., 25, 26 & 27.

Lexikon de Ägyptologie (six vols) ed. Wolfgang Helck, Eberhard Otto, and Wolfhart Westendorf (Wiesbaden: O. Harrassowitz, 1972)

Leiris, Michel (1958) *La Possession et ses aspects théatraux chez le Ethipeins de Gondar*, Paris

Lewis, I M (1971) *Ecstatic Religion*, Penguin books.

Messing, Simon (1958) 'Group therapy and social sta tus in the Zar cult of Ethiopia' *American Anthropologist* 60 pp 1120-7.

Lichtheim, Miriam (1980) *Ancient Egyptian Literature*, 3 vols, University of California Press.

Littmann, Enno (1950) *Arabische Geisterbeschwörungen aus Ägypten*, Harrassowitz Verlag, Leipzig

Logan, JJ (1990) 'The Origins of the Jmy-wt fetish', *JARCE* 27, pp 61-70

Luft, Ulruch (1986) Götitnger Miszellen 92 for feast dates

Mercer, S A B (1949) *The Religion of Ancient Egypt*, London, London, Luzac 1949).

Metcalf P & Huntington, W R (1979) *Celebrations of Death*, CUP NY

Morgan, M (2005) *Tankhem, Seth and Egyptian Magick*, Mandrake of Oxford.

Morgan, C (2002) *Medicine of the Gods: basic principles of Ayurvedic medicine*, Mandrake.

Morgan, M (2006) *The Bull of Ombos: Seth and Egyptian magick II*, Mandrake.

Nabarz, Payam (2005) *The Mysteries of Mithras: The Pagan Belief That Shaped the Christian World*, USA.

Neugebauer O (1949) 'The Early History of the Astrolabe' *Isis* 40, pp.240-256.

Neugebauer O & Parker, R (1962) Ancient Egyptian Astronomical Texts, 4 vols, Brown University.
I. Early Decans
II. Ramesside Star Clocks

III. Decans, Planets, Constellations & Zodiacs
IV. Plates.

Nicholson P T & Shaw I, (2000) *Ancient Egyptian Materials and Technology*, Cambridge.

Nilsson, Martin P (1920) *Primitive Time Reckoning* , Lund.

Parker, Richard A (1950) *The Calendars of Ancient Egypt*, Chicago.

Parker, Richard A (1959) *Vienna Demotic Papyri on Luna Omina*, Brown University.

Parker, Richard A (1962) *A Saite Oracle Papyrus from Thebes (Papyrus Brooklyn 47.218.3)* Brown University

Pinch, G (1993) *Votive Offerings to Hathor*, Oxford

Pinch, Geraldine (1994) *Magic in Ancient Egypt*, British Museum Press.

Plutarch, *On Isis and Osiris*, Greek with English translation by Gwyn Griffiths, Cardiff.

Preisendanz, Karl (1928 & 1931) *Papyri Graecae Magicae*, 2 Vols, Leipzig. Reprinted Stuttgart 1973-4)

Ghalioungui, P (1965) Magic & Medical Science in Anceint Egypt, Hodder & Stoughton.

Reiner, Erica (1975-), with David Pingree, *Babylonian Planetary Omens*, (The Enuma Anu Enlil) Brill/Styx.
Vol II Fasc 1 Venus Tablet of Ammisaduga (1975)
Vol II Fasc 2 Constellations (1981)
Vol III: Venus Omens (1998)
Vol IV: Jupiter Omens (2005)

Reymond, E A E (1969) *The Mythological Origin of the Egyptian Temple*, Manchester University Press.

Ritner, R K (1990) 'Ostracon Gardiner 363 - a spell against night terrors.' *JARCE* 27 25-41.

Ritner, R K (1993) *The Mechanics of Ancient Egyptian Magical Practice*, Chicago.

Ritner, R K (1996) 'Dream Oracles' in Hallo, William W, *The Context of Scripture* Vol I, Brill.

Roberts, A (1995) *Hathor Rising, the serpent power of Ancient Egypt*, Northgate

Rose, Lyne (1999) *Sun, Moon & Sothis: a study of calendars & calendar reforms in Ancient Egypt*.

Samuel D & Bolt P (1995) 'Rediscovering Ancient Egyptian Beer', *Brewer's Guardian UK*, December pp27-32.

Schott, S (1950) *Altägyptische Festdaten*, Wiesbaden.

Servajean, F (2004) 'Lune ou Soleil d'or un Épisode des aventures 'Horus et de Seth (P Chester Beatty I R° 11 1-13 1)' *Revue D'Égyptologie*, Tome 55, pp125-148.

Shaw, Ian (1995) *Dictionary of Ancient Egypt*, BM. 'priest'

Shorter, Alan W (1935), 'The God Nehebkau', JEA XXi pp47sq

Spalinger, A (1991) 'An unexpected source in a festival calendar' RdeE 41.

Spalinger, A (1992) *Three Studies of Egyptian Feasts and their chronological implications* - Baltimore, USA.

Spalinger, A (1993) 'A chronological analysis of the feast of *thy*' *Studien Zur Altägyptischer Culture* 20, pp289-303.

Spalinger, A (1994) *Revolutions in Time: Studies in Ancient Egyptian Calendrics*, Van Siclen Books, Texas.

Stadelmann, R (1967) *Syrisch-palästinensische Gottheiten in Ägypten*, Leiden.

Te Velde (1967) *Seth: God of Confusion: a study of his role in Egyptian Mythology and Religion*, E J Brill (rev 1977).

Te Velde (1970) 'The God Heka in Egyptian Theology' *JEOL* 21 175-186 followed by unnumbered plate section.

Troy, L (1987) 'Have a nice day!' in *The Religion of the Ancient Egyptians - Cognitive Structures*, Proceedings of Symposia in Uppsala & Bergen (ed) Englund, G, pp.127 [316 Upp].

Versnel, H. S.(2002) 'The Poetics of the Magical Charm : An Essay on the Power of Words.' In *Magic and Ritual in the Ancient World*, edited by Paul Allan Mirecki and Marvin W. Meyer, 105-58. Leiden: E. J. Brill, 2002.

Vernus, (1981), 'Omina Calendérique et comptabilité d'offrandes sur une tablette Hiératique de la XVIIIe Dynastie' RdeE, vol 33 pp89-124.Pap Leyden I 346.

Van Dijk, J (1986) " 'Anath, Seth and the Seed of Ra" in Hospers, J H, *Scripta Sigma Vocis*, Gronigen

Van Walsen (1982) 'Month names and feast at Deir el-Medina' in *Gleanings from Deir el-Medina* eds Memaree & Janssen, pp. 214-46, Leiden.

Von Bomhard, Anne-Sophie *The Egyptian Calendar*, Periplus 1999.

Wainwright, G A (1923) 'The Red Crown in Early prehistoric times', *JEA* 9, pp26-33.

Wainwright, G A (1938) *The Sky Religion in Egypt: its antiquity and effects*, Cambridge.

Wainwright, G A (1932) 'Letopolis', *JEA 19* pp. 164-167

Wainwright, G A (1935), 'Celestial Associations of Min', *JEA* 21 pp.152-170.

Wells, R A (1985) 'The Satet Temple on Elephantine: an Egyptian Stonehenge' SAK 12 pp274

Wells, R A (1990) 'Ra and the Calendars', in Spalinger (1994).

Glossary

Acacia: tree associated with Seth and Osiris. An artifact in the Metropolitan Museum of Art shows Tawaret (Hippo), together with Mut (Mother) emerging from an Acacia. The seed pods have an astringent, antibacteriological properties and were used in Egyptian medicine for uterine complaints and infections. (see Allen J P 2005)

Alexandrian calendar has an additional epagomenal day every four years to arrest the forward shift of dates.

Amon: originally a wind deity, who rises in Ramesside theology, to be, together with Ra, King of the Gods, much as in later hermetic theology, the 'pantocrator' stands above the 'lesser' gods. Prototype is represented as a human being (at times ithyphallic), wearing a mortarboard crowned with two plumes or, at times, with a ram's head, the animal dedicated to him. With the goddess Mut and the god Khonsu, they formed the Theban Triad. He was also identified with the god Ra and venerated under the name of Amon-Ra. The cult's principal location was in Thebes.

Anath: Canaanite-Phoenician goddess of fertility and victory

Ankh-tawi: Necropolis near Memphis, Ptah, south-of-his-wall was lord of Ankhtawy, Bast was called Lady of Ankhtawy

Anubis: a jackal-headed god who presided over mummification and accompanied the dead to the hereafter.

Apep, Apophis, demon of non-being, the opponent of Ra. His companions referred to as the 'children of Bedesh' and 'children of the storm' in Cairo Calendar

Astarte: Canaanite goddess, called *Lady of Heaven* by the Egyptians.

Atef: the double-feathered crown of Osiris

Ba: 'soul' – after death, the person live on in this form not on earth but in the tomb and the community's memory. Ba is the characteristic manifestation of a entiry, divine or human. Bears comparison with Hindu: 'Linga'.

Barque of the Millions of Years: Ra's Manjet boat, with which he sailed through the 12 provinces of day. For his night journeys, Ra used his Mesket boat.

Bebon (*b3b3wj*) also Baba:.Baboon god and demon of sexual potency and prowess with red ears and features of Seth. Names in various texts including Plutarch and Almanacs of Lucky & Unlucky Days. See Kees, Horus & Seth II 47-48

Bousiris: from the Egyptian, meaning 'City of Osiris'. A city in Lower Egypt where the worship of Osiris was born.

Castles for millions of years: On the west bank of the Nile at Thebes, the Pharaohs of the 18th, 19th and 20th Dynasties had large religious monuments built, which were improperly called 'funerary temples'. In reality, they used them, during their lifetime, to worship the deified pharaoh associated with Amon, the main Theban deity.

Chaîne Opératoire - methological concept devised in the 1960s by André Leroi-Gourhan in which the sequence of construction and deconstruction is analysed for information about the culture behind an artefact.

Cheth = CTh or Seth in etc. A secret name of power.

Cippus: Latin term meaning post or stake. In archaeology: 'a small low column, sometimes without a base or capital and most frequently bearing an inscription.' (OED: Gwily, J ,1842, An Enclyclopedia of Architecture: historical, theoretic and practical.) Used in Egyptology in reference to the Horus 'Cippi' - an image of 'Horus among the crocodiles.' The inscription describes an episode whereby Isis, during their sojourn in the Delta marshes hiding from Seth, cures the infant Horus of the effects of scorpion bite. Water collected in these Cippi is considered magically potent to ward off the effects of scorpion stings.

Coffin Texts: a term reserved for those spells which are peculiar to the early coffins and do not recur later, not at least until the Saite period, when some of them were sporadically revived. These Coffin Texts contain excerpts from the earliest Pyramid Texts, usurped by the nobility of the IX-XI dynasties for their own benefit (Gardiner: 1927:13).

Critical edition: a special edition of a text, edited from several sources to produce a final scholarly edition. This so-called 'critical edition' may not correspond with any of the extant 'street' editions of a text, and for this reason is viewed by some as a distortion.

Cubit: approximately half a metre

Damanhur: 'Town of Horus', argued by some to be the original Behadit in the western delta, until its transfer to Edfu as the 'Behadit' of Upper Egypt.

Dead (western): the Land of the Setting Sun: this is the Kingdom of the Dead.

Dendara: the capital of the sixth Nome of Upper Egypt, and its necropolis contains tombs dug between the predynastic period and the end of the Old Kingdom. This site's renown is due to the famous Temple of Hathor, which dates back to the Greco-

Roman period. Dendara was dedicated to Hathor, one of the oldest Egyptian deities, represented as a cow or a woman with cow's ears.

Decan: 36 stars on the belt of the southern ecliptic, whose rising was used to mark the passage of the 'hours' during each cycle or 'week' of ten days.

Egyptian: A language of the Hamiti-Semitic group which includes Semitic, Berber, Cushitic and Hausa)

Epagomenal: see Intercalary.

Ennead: (*psdt*) 'The company of heaven', 'companions of the sun & moon', A group of more or less nine deities, such as the company of *Heliopolis* - Atum, Shu and Tefnut, Geb and Nut, Osiris and Isis, Seth, Nephthys.

Êsenephus = *s.t-nb.t ḥw.t* = Isis & Nephthys - in 'garbled' version of PGM

Griffin: The griffin is an important avatar of Seth appearing on talismanic wands made from hippo ivory - the name is 'teshtesh' in Middle Egyptian. Leibovitch once remarked: 'that as "dieu sauveur" Seth is a griffin. On the one hand the griffin is a guardian angel, on the other an avenger, pursuing its enemies at furious speed or crushing them underfoot, as appears from the many illustrations in the articles by Leibovitch. It might be that at Beni Hasan these two functions are divided over the falcon-headed griffin and the Seth-animal, and that the occurrence of griffins with a falcon's head or the head of the Seth-animal is not altogether arbitrary, but is connected with the duality of the gods Horus and Seth in mythology.' J. Leibovitch, *Le griffon I*, BIE 25 (1943), p. 188 and fig. 5 quoted in Te Velde.

Harpoon: the main weapons used for hunting hippos.

Head: 'reserve', a substitute for the mummy's head, placed in the tomb of the deceased in case the latter is destroyed (see Hayes 1953 : 109).

Histeriola: divine precedent for a spell.

Hathor: cow-headed deity (sometimes depicted as a woman with cow's ears) protected women and the dead, as she was likened to the Goddess of the Kingdom of the Dead; she was also goddess of music and intoxication.

Horus: god of the sky and protector of the pharaoh to whom he was likened. Horus could be depicted as a falcon-headed man. As the son of Osiris and Isis, he was often represented as infant (Harpocrates) with a finger held to his lips; a gesture rather paradoxically interpreted in the Hermetic Order of the Golden Dawn, as 'the sign of silence.'

Iathath = (ie Seth). In the Greek Magical Papyrus (Betz 1986). The black 'blood' of Seth.

Ideogramme: a pictorial sign, that has no phonetic value but nevertheless helps define the meaning or sense rather than the sound of a word. Incidentally where the ideogramme follows one or more phonogrammes and ends the word, it is known as a determinative. The ideogrammes are historically the oldest part of the Egyptian language, the phonograms later prefixed to it for the sake of clarity (Gardiner 1926).

Intercalary: twelve lunar months of 30 days equals 360, which leaves five extra or intercalary days, on which the priests of Heliopolis assigned the birth of five gods, almost as a supplement to their own theological system. The five gods said to be born on these days were: Osiris, Isis, Seth, Nephthys and Horus the child. This schema is known from Pyramid Text 1961 and Plutarch, *Isis and Osiris*, 12. Mercer (1949 : 277) states that the priests of Heliopolis had invented this calendar by 2781BC.

Ipet Hemet: Hippo or perhaps Hathor?

Jeu, Books of and Jeu the Hieroglyphist of the so-called 'Headless One' ritual of PGM (known in contemporary magick variously as the 'Bornless One', 'Liber Samech' and 'Preliminary Invocation of the Goetia') . *The Books of Jeu* are Coptic / Gnostic texts found at Nag Hammadi.

Kiki: seemingly the burning oil from the castor oil plant (ricinus communis) used in lamps.

Khmun: Hermopolis Magna in Middle Egypt, cult centre of Thoth.

Ladder of Seth: means by which the king's soul rises to the stars. Made of iron that has fallen from the heavens. Jacob's ladder may also be a meteorite (see Wainwright).

LPH: abreviation used by Egyptologists for stative formula: 'Life, Prosperity and Health' - $3nḫ(w)$ $wḏ3(w)$ $snb(w)$ - 'alive, sound and healthy' or 'Life, prosperity and health' in older translations.

Maat heru: speaking true, which will get you through the gates after judgement.

Maat: divine personification of the cosmic order, secondarily connected to the concepts of truth and justice. She wears an ostrich plume on her head, the transcription of her name.

Min: in origin a sky god - one of whose forms is as a white bull tethered to axial pillar as cult object.

Mut: the wife of Amon, she was venerated in Thebes. Originally depicted as a vulture, she later took on a human form.

Neolithic: of or relating to the cultural period of the Stone Age beginning around 10,000BC in the Middle East and later elsewhere, characterized by the development of agriculture and the making of polished stone implements.

Neter: god or the divine.

Nehes: Nubia; (later Kash: Kush), according to Baynes & Malek (2000) the derivation of 'Nubia' may be from 'Nub' - meaning gold.

Neith: goddess of the hunt and war, whose cult centre was at Sais.

Nome: one of forty-two administrative districts, significantly also the number of the judges of the dead. Interestingly each Nome coincides with one of the enormous temporary lakes caused by the annual Nile flood (Butzer 1976).

Nomen: the King's titulary consisted of five great names. The family name, called the nomen by Egyptologists, is introduced by epithet 'son of Ra'.

On: Heliopolis

Onnophris: Osiris as known in the tradition of the magical papyri and Christianity, about whom is said: He brings peace to the lands in his name of Sokaris, mighty is his reputation in his name of Osiris, he persists until the ends of eternity in his name Onnophris.

Onomastica: words lists detailing divinity and geography. See final book of Apuleus' *Golden Ass* for an example, where it says her true name only known to the Egyptians and Ethiopians.

Onuris: Anhur, god of hunt and war, resident at This. He returns the Eye of the Sun as his consort Mehit.

Osiris: the husband of Isis; after having been killed by his brother, Seth, he fathered a son, Horus, who, grown to adulthood, avenged him. He is represented with his crown (atef), his scepter (bequa), and his flail, (nekhekh).

Pronomen: King's first cartouche or throne name.

Pars pro toto: 'part stands for the whole'. Ie type of time reckoning based on the observation of a single event to represent the whole cycle. For example the Slavonic *Leto* means the 'summer' and 'year'. It may seem obvious to us in temperate climes that there is only one summer per year, and therefore we could say 'she is a maid of eighteen summers' and we would all understand that.. But in some equatorial regions there is no winter or summer and there are two wet seasons! Some old traditions ignore or lump together whole segments of the year - hence the old Roman year of ten months.

Petosis: an Hellenistic astrologer who made an association between the Northern Constellations and the Lunar days. Source: Neugebauer & Parker (1962 III : 216). Most reference books say this Petosis is the occupant of the famous Hermopolitan 4th century BC tomb, but N&P cast doubt on this and indeed the theories of Petosis. The late text to which they refer is not quoted in their monumental work but may be in Neugebauer's 'Egyptian Planetary Texts' *Transactions of the American Philosophical Society*, Vol XXXII part II, Jan 1942 209-50.

PDM = Papyri Demotika Magicae

PGM = Papyri Graecae Magicae – Preisendanz's (qv) sobriquet, although he omitted the Demotic spells as of less interest and therefore ensured they disappeared from scholarly discourse for the best part of a century.

Pharaoh: Egyptian word for king is 'nsw' - 'pharaoh', as used in the Hebrew Bible is probably derived from 'per'o' - king's house.

Preisendanz, Karl, editor of the PGM in two volumes, 1928 & 1931.

Pre-Harakhti: a combination of Re and Horus!

Ptah: the God of Memphis, brought the universe into being along with the hieroglyphic pictogrammes, the most primitive level of the Egyptian language. These were later simplified and reduced to a short list of alphabetic signs by Thoth, the god of scribes. Ptah, the husband of the Lion Goddess, Sekhmet, was depicted wearing a mummy's shroud, holding in his hand a scepter. He was later likened to another Memphis god of death, Sokaris, and was worshipped in his syncretic form of Ptah-Sokaris.

Pylon: a monumental temple entrance, consisting of a portal between two enormous trapezoidal monoliths.

Ra, or Re, as Egyptian sun-god Ra. Ra was beholden to Seth for defending him against the demons who assailed him on his daily journey through the skies.

Rekhyt: the plebs, others say the followers of Seth

Sais: centre in western delta, where local rulers, decendents of 25th dynasty, became important in the conflicts of the 8th century BCE.

Sekhem: 'power', 'sign of power' hence 'image' or 'statue'. The Ba (qv) returns or is installed in the mummy / corpse / statue giving power. Assmann discussed this in relation to the hermetic doctrine 'as above, so below'.

Sekhmet: lion-headed goddess, sometimes crowned with the

solar disk. She protected the royal power; she can be likened to Hathor, Bastet and Isis.

Shed: 'save', 'rescue', 'saviour' - used especially after the traumas of the Amarna period. The Egyptian aspect of the semitic god Reshef - or young saviour god used as an epithet of Horus.

Shen: the coil of rope known by the french term 'cartouche' - the Egyptian term derived from word meaning to encircle. Symbol of eternity and protective device around the name of the king.

Sycamore, Lady of the Southern: epithet of Hathor at Memphis, she had assisted Horus when blinded by Seth.

Tê: the underworld

Teshtesh (see Griffin)

Thebes: during the 18th Dynasty (ca.1550 - 1295BC), the city of Weset was founded by Amenhotep I; better known by its Greek name, Thebes, it became the heart of the country. It was at this time that the Great Temple of Amon in Karnak became the country's most important religious centre and the royal necropolises were excavated in the Valley of the Kings and the Valley of the Queens. *Theban Triad*: Amon-Ra, Mut and Khonsu.

Index

Symbols

12 provinces of day 254

A

Aa-pehetey 205
   'great of strength' 205
Aabt-offerings 159
Aaner 205
   'great of fear' 205
Abydos 143, 148, 215
   Formula 90
Africa
   East 175
   Loango 175
   Massai 175
Age
   Neolithic 180
Aion 218
Akes 205
Akhet 143
Akhw. *See also* spirits (akhw)
Almanac of Lucky & Unlucky Days 130, 137, 144, 157, 162
Amenhotep I 151, 262
Amon 253
Amseti 208
Amuletic Decrees 154
Amulets 159
Amun 24, 25, 146, 151, 153, 156, 192
Anat 253
Anhur 259
Ankh 202, 253
Ankh-tawi 253
Anubis 79, 150, 253
Apophis 149, 253. *See also* children: children of Bedesh (Apophis)
Artemis 129

Ass. *See* donkey
Associated 89
Astarte 254
Astrology 149
Astronomical ceiling 172, 191
Ate 254
Athyr 147
Atlantis 196

B

Baba/Babai 254
Baboon
   Babai
      red eared Baboon. *See also* Baba/Babai
Babylon
   Enuma Anu Enlil 217
   lunar calendar 187
Bahr Yusuf 164
Banebdjedet 254
Bastet 149, 151, 262
Bebon 254
Beer 144, 254
Berber 256
Bes 218
Betelgeuse 181
Bible
   Leviticus 184
Birth
   conception 182
   nine months 181
Black 159
Blood 257
Blue Lily (Nymphaea caerulea) 50, 204
Boat 254
Book of Days, the Egyptian 130
Book of Gates 180
Book of Nut 73

Book of Revelation 219
Book of the Law 163
Borchardt, Ludwig 167, 192
Brugsch, Heinrich 165, 167, 176, 191
Bubastis 129, 151
Bull
  Mes 194
  of Meroe 254
Bull of Ombos 40, 163, 179, 193, 197, 202
Busiris 129, 254
Buto 129

C

Calendar
  Civil 164
  Gregorian 139, 166
  Jewish 186
    Adar II 186
    Nisan II 186
  Julian 133, 139, 140, 184, 185
  Lunar 164, 172, 174, 176, 192, 236
    archaic 193
    calibrating 185
    calibration 38
    Southern 179
  Lunar double dates 165
  Lunar-Solar 179, 180
  Lunar-Sothic 185
  Lunar-Stella 130, 167, 184
Cannibal Hymn 153
Canopic jars 200, 254
Cartouche 254
Cattle. *See* Bata
Choiak 27, 28, 147, 148
Cleopatra 95
Cloth
  linen 143
Clothing 131, 146, 150
Coffin
  texts **255**

Constantius 219
Constellations
  Cygnus 181
  Milky Way 182
  Orion 181
Corn mummy 89. *See also* Neper
Craftsmen 147
Crown
  Atef 254, 260
Cup 204
Cygnus 183

D

Dakhleh 153, 171, 213
  Stele 215, 216
Damanhur 255
Dance. *See also* Zar
Day
  break 180
  epagomenal 22, 137, 157, 159
Dead. the 255
Death
  embalming 28, 148
Decans 79, 131, 149, 193, 208
Deir el Bahri 156, 180, 187, 191
Deir el Haggar 171, 213
Deir el Medina 131, 151
Dendara 140, 144, 255
  Mistress of 27, 147
Depuydt, Leo 37, 164, 186
Disease & medicine 168
Divination. *See* omens
Djed pillars 148, 256
Dreams. *See* evil: sleep
  incubation 218
Drunkenness 144, 152
  feast of 187
Duamutef 200, 206, 208
Duat 180, 182

E

Earth 196
Ebers, George 168
Edfu 140, 198, 255

Egg 79
El Lahun 164
El Sabbai. Sherif, Temple Festivals &
    Calendars of 174
Elephantine 179
Enitef 202
Ennead 193, 257
Epagomenal days 256. *See also*
    children: children of Nut
    (epagomenal days)
Epiphi 155
Equinox
    Vernal 181
Esna 154
Eye
    equip 212

F

Faiyum 164
Feasts/festivals
    attendence 152
    Fire (Rekh-nedes) 73, 79, 149,
        150
    Fire (Rekh-wer) 150
    Great 149
    individual 137
    of heaven 135
    political 137
    regional feasts 137
    seizing the staffs 154
    thirty spears 149
    Valley 155
Feeding
    the gods. *See also* eating
Fertility 147
Fetish 215
Fire
    Isle of 153
    walking. *See also* feasts/festivals
Flail 260
Flint
    mooring post 194
Folk. *See also* Rekhyt

G

Geb 208
    and Nuit 196
Gemini 181
Ghosts. *See also* Akhw
Goddess 105
Gods
    accursed 197
    Company of Heaven 193
Gold 259
Graphiti 218
    proskynema 218
Greek Magical Papyris 212
Greeks
    Hellenic 196
    Hellenistic 196, 208
Green 21, 159

H

Hadit 207
    hall of the magician' 207
Hakow 202
Hamlet 197
Hapy 200, 208
Harpokrates 257
Hathor 26, 40, 57, 140, 147,
        149, 153, 172, 200, 215,
        255, 257
    seven 215
Hatshepsut 180, 187, 191, 194
Hausa 256
Hawk 147
Hekayet 58
Heliopolis 157, 179, 196
Heptagram 90
Hepui 205
Herbs 168
Hermopolis 123
Herodotus 129, 151, 154, 155,
        193, 212
Hinduism
    Tantrism 183
Hippopotamus 105, 154, 172,

193, 197
Histeriola 257
Horizon 180
Horus 28, 148, 158, 197, 202, 204, 208, 216, 257
  & Seth 154
  be praised 205
  Behadit 255
  Edfu 27, 147, 149, 194, 208
  Four Sons 200
  Hekenew 205
  new moon 38, 217
  the Elder 22, 157
Horus & Seth
  conflict of 197
  contending 193
House of Life 43, 166
Hu/Hw 22, 157
Hymn
  danced 53

I

Iathath 257
Ibis 205
Ideogramme 257
Illahun 164, 166
Imsety 200
Ipet 105, 156, 171, 172
Irem-awa 203
Iren-djedef 202
Iren-renef-djesef 202
Iron 258
Isis 22, 93, 157, 158, 193, 194, 197, 200, 208

J

Jackal 79, 205
John Barleycorn 148
John Soanes museum 180

K

Karnak 24, 95, 146, 156, 262
Kebehsenuf 202

Khentykhet 100
Khmun 258
Khnum 219
Khonsu 95, 140, 153, 156, 253
  wanderer 153
Kiki 256
King 206
Knife 202
Kom Ombo 153
Kush 256

L

Ladder
  Jacob's 258
Lady of Heaven 254
Lakes
  temporary 259
Letopolis 15, 158
Letters to the Dead 154
Library
  Alexandria 140
License to depart 86
Luxor 24, 146, 191

M

Ma-enitef 202
Maat 63, 100, 258
  Maat heru - speaking true 258
Magic. *See* eating: magick
  body 182
  heka 203
  mistress of 158
Mandulis 218
Manjet boat 254
Mantis 219
Mastabas 38
Mechir 150
Medinet Habu 154
Megiddo 165
Mehet 207
Mehit 259
Mesket boat 254
Mesore 156, 165, 179
Meteorites 258

Min 50, 67, 154
Month
  dark third week 206
  first day of 176
  gods of 191
  intercalary 157, 185, 187
  lunar 175, 236
  names 132
  straddle 186
  synodic 174
  Tekhy 40
  theophoric 139, 168
Moon 120
  anomaly 175
  bio-dynamism 168
  blue 167
  bright or waxing half 196
  conjunction 174
  dark or waning half 166, 197, 203
  day of rams 203
  festivals 194
  first visibility 38
  full 26, 27, 38, 145, 147, 172, 213
  gods of the waxing 196
  lunar days 194
  mansions 236
  new 27, 38, 147, 150, 165, 174, 176
    determining 185
  old crescent 175
  sight 220
  white nights 132, 172
Motherhood. *See also* birth
Mummy
  cloth 150
Mut 24, 146, 149, 153, 156, 253, 258

N

Nagada 179, 184, 185
  Ombos 193
Narcotic. *See* Blue Lily (Nymphaea caerulea)
Nature 138
Necropolis 262
Nehebkau 148
Nehes 203, 205, 259
Neith 67, 261
Nekhekh - flail 260
Neper 89, 152
  corn mummy 152
Nephthys 22, 57, 157, 158, 197, 208
  Beautiful of face 158
Nepthys 43
Neterew 259
Neuserre 150
Nile 179
  first cataract 179
  High 138
  inundation 27, 147
Nilsson, Martin
  Primitive Time Reckoning 167
Niuserre 146
Nome 259
nomen 259
None 38
Nubia 259
Nuit 73, 180, 181, 182, 208
  cosmic winds 172
  Milky Way 181

O

Observation 166
  error 175
Ombos. *See* Nagada
Omens 212
  crescent moon 217
  Lunar 212, 213
On 259
Onnophris in Sais 259
Onuris 207, 259
Opening the Mouth 150, 204
Opet 145
Oracles 215, 218. *See also* omens
  Judgement Stele 214

knuckle bone 219
Potter 219
Osireion 218
Osiris 22, 63, 143, 144, 147, 152, 157, 163, 171, 197, 260
   as vanished moon 28, 148
   decapitation 215
Ostrich 258
Oxyrhynchus 171

P

Pachons 152
Pagan 138, 218
   inclusive nature 217
Palermo stone 50
Pan 154
Panopolis 50
Papremis 129, 154
Papyrus 131
Papyrus Carlsberg 187
Papyrus Ebers 167, 168, 170, 173
   calendar 169
Papyrus, Edwin Smith Surgical Papyrus 168
Papyrus Harris Magical 79
Papyrus Kahun 164
Papyrus Reisner 131, 159
Papyrus Vandier 79
Parker, Richard 167, 176, 191
Payni 154
Peret 148
Pesedjenet 165, 176
Petosiris 193, 206
Phallus 50
   erect 253
Phaophi 150
Pharmenoth 150
Pharmuthi 172
Priest 164
   overseer of the hour 166
Priestess 25, 146
   God's Wife 25, 146
Prophets 53
   Christian 219
Ptah 146, 150, 261
Ptolemaic 140, 144, 153, 194
Pylon 261

Q

Qadesh 165
Qebehsenuf 208

R

Ra 110, 149, 157, 261
   birth of 183
   Pre 261
   Pre-Harakhti 261
   sun god 181
RaHorakhty 110, 159, 186
Ramesses II 187
Red
   celestial pole 194
   hoofs 194
   letter days 139
   ochre 218
Rennutet 89, 140, 151, 152
Ritual
   Timing for 38
Rome 196

S

Sais 67, 255, 257, 259
Satet 179
Scepter 260
   Was 202
Scorpion 149
Seasons 134
   Akhet 24, 145, 147, 150
   Peret 150
   Shemu 152, 154, 155
Sed 144, 154
Sekhmet 148, 149, 261
Selket 149
Semitic 256
Senmut 187, 194, 197, 202, 203
Sepermeru 203

Serapis 218
Seth 22, 40, 43, 58, 79, 130, 149, 153, 157, 158, 163, 172, 193, 197, 202, 203, 205, 208, 213, 219. *See also* Horus & Seth
    Apophis 154
    Companions of 206, 236
    feasts **172**
    Full Moon 38, 217
    ladder of 258
    Mercury / Imy-sha 194
    temple of 203
    'Who is in the god's Booth' 205
Sethians 138, 197, 208, 215
Sety I 180
Severed head 215
Sex
    incest 154
"Sexualized" minerals 93
Shakespeare 197
Shecha. *See also* Zar: cults
Shed 262
Shed-Keru 205
Shu 74, 196, 208
    & Tefnut
        death of 196
    moisture 196
Sickle (Kapesh) 53
Sirius. *See* Sopdu (Sirius)
Sistrum (zeSzeS) 147, 202
Sixt 38
Sixteen 213. *See also* day of rams
    day of lunar month 38, 213
    sun and moon 213
Sky 196
    raising of 151
Sleep. *See* evil: sleep
Snake 89, 151
    demon 149
Sobek 153
Sokar 63, 147, 148, 259, 261
Solstice
    summer orientation 180
    winter 179, 181, 183
    winter orientation 180
Songs
    drinking 25, 146
Sopdu (Sirius) 139, 167, 179, 181, 185
    Heliacal Rising 38, 179, 181, 184, 185
    heliacal rising of 135
    Heliacal Rising of Sirius 138
    Sothic cycle 174
Sosipatra 219
Sothis. *See* Sopdu (Sirius)
Spirits (akhw). *See* Akhw
Star
    70 days absence 184
    apparent motion 175
    clock 180
    Rigel 181
Stele Panakht. *See also* Akhw: Panacht Stele
Stonehenge 175
Summer 152, 154, 155
Sun
    god 40. *See also* Ra
Sycamore 262

T

Talmis 218
Tanen 67
Tankhem 202, 236
Taweret 106
Tefnut 196, 208
Tekenu 204
Tekhen 187
Terce 38
Thebes 253, 262
Thoth 120, 130, 139, 143, 186, 187
Thutmose III 165
Trapezoid 261
Tum 208
Tutu 172
Tybi 148
Typhon. *See also* Seth

Typhonian 172, 197

U

Ursa Major *43*. *See* Great Bear
Uto 149

V

Valley of the Kings 262
Valley of the Queens 262
Venomous 89
Vessel divination 79
Voice
   oracles 218

W

Wag 130, 143, 145, 164
Wepwawet 79
Weset 262
Wind 196
Winter 150, 151
Work 131

Y

Year
   365 day 184
   eleven day interval 185
   leap 138, 139, 187
   month pairing 167
   new 23, 137, 143
   nineteen year cycle 187
   opener of 185, 186
   Solar-Sothic 185
   virtual 138
   wandering 138, 156, 184

Z

Zodiac 140

Spot any mistakes or want to offer some constructive feedback? The subject matter of this book is complex and inevitably there will be errors of transcription and understanding. In addition some of the ritual material undergoes natural revision by repeated use. Contact the author via the publishers and in return receive an update on work in progress, access to revisions plus a free gift.

Write C/O

Mandrake of Oxford
PO Box 250
OXFORD
OX1 1AP (UK)

Or search for Mandrake or Mogg Morgan on the Internet.

www.ingramcontent.com/pod-product-compliance
Lightning Source LLC
Chambersburg PA
CBHW031138160426
43193CB00008B/176